Pathfinder® Guides

C000054192

Thames Valley and Chilterns

Walks

Compiled by
Nick Channer

Contents

At-a-glance

Comments

Pleasant walking by the Thames and the chance to explore an interesting old town are the chief ingredients of this short and easy walk.

Watlington Hill provides extensive views across the Oxfordshire Plain and is the starting point for this short but highly enjoyable walk.

Much of the route of this walk is through the splendid woodlands of Burnham Beeches, a delight at any time of the year.

Berkshire's surprisingly isolated and dramatic south-west corner is the setting for this very pleasant walk offering good views of the spectacular rolling downland on the county's border with Hampshire.

There are grand views over the Thames Valley from Wittenham Clumps, plus attractive riverside meadows and a fine medieval abbey to visit.

After a pleasant meander along a leafy stretch of the historic Kennet & Avon Canal, the route explores peaceful paths and tracks in the secluded Kennet valley.

This walk takes you across part of the open and largely empty chalk downs that lie to the west of the Thames Valley and are in stark contrast to the wooded Chilterns.

Ancient grazing land beside Britain's most famous river, the Thames – or Isis, provides the picturesque backdrop to this easy, undemanding walk, a stone's throw from Oxford city centre.

A pleasant walk through the attractive rural surroundings of Oxford. One of the highlights is a visit to Jarn Mound, built in the early 1930s by a noted archaeologist.

There are fine views across the valley and some splendid riverside walking beside the Thames between Hurley and Marlow.

The first half of the route to Cookham is mostly across meadows and marshland; the second half is along Cliveden Reach, one of the finest stretches of the Thames.

There is plenty of attractive woodland walking and towards the end grand views across the Thames Valley to the Berkshire Downs.

Starting high above Oxfordshire and Wiltshire, this impressive walk explores a land of romantic mythology and ancient prehistoric sites. All this and the Ridgeway thrown in for good measure.

The walk takes you through a surprisingly remote Chilterns landscape, passing by the interesting and relatively isolated churches at Great Hampden and Little Hampden.

After following the Thames around a long bend, the route climbs to a grand viewpoint above the river. A pleasant walk with only gentle climbs and fine views over the Thames Valley.

There are two attractive villages, the fine town of Abingdon and lengthy, enjoyable stretches of walking beside the Thames.

This walk links a well-known riverside town and an attractive Chilterns village. There are fine views and the last part hugs the banks of the Thames along the famous regatta course.

Plenty of variety and historic interest on this walk that includes the riverside meadows where Magna Carta was signed, part of Windsor Great Park and distant views of the great castle.

The middle stage of this walk explores the upper Thames, a very different river in both character and appearance above Oxford, with two delightful Cotswold villages at either end.

This route combines superb views from the Chilterns escarpment with some highly enjoyable walking through the beautiful and extensive woodlands of the Ashridge Estate.

The walk takes you through a typical Chilterns landscape and includes two attractive villages with fine medieval churches.

A classic walk that includes one of the most magnificent viewpoints on the Chilterns escarpment, some splendid wooded stretches and a view of Chequers.

There are glimpses of the Thames before this attractive walk reaches the unspoilt village of Mapledurham, regularly used as a film and television location. The return leg is via pretty countryside in the southern Chilterns.

Between the three great country houses passed on this walk, there are some grand stretches of woodland and superb views over the Chilterns from a ridge-top path.

You walk through a rolling landscape of well-wooded dry valleys and about half way round pass one of the most interesting churches in the Chilterns.

This lengthy walk covers woodland, including part of the outstanding Chipperfield Common, and riverside, linking four villages in the attractive Chess valley.

A walk across the open expanses of the Berkshire Downs is followed by a delightful stretch beside the Thames. At the end you climb to a superb viewpoint above the river.

This walk is through a Chilterns landscape at its finest. It includes three villages, a pleasant town and a magnificent view from the escarpment of Chinnor Hill.

Keymap

Introduction to the Thames Valley and the Chilterns

The Chilterns form part of the long line of chalk hills stretching intermittently across southern and eastern England, in a roughly north-east to northerly direction from Wiltshire to the Yorkshire coast. They are both the highest and most distinctive part of that chain, extending from the Thames Valley across Oxfordshire, Buckinghamshire, Hertfordshire and Bedfordshire, before petering out in the flatter country around Luton. To the south and west they are bordered by the Thames, on the other side of which the chalk hills continue as

the Berkshire Downs. The chief contrast between the Berkshire Downs and the Chilterns is that the former mainly comprise open, rolling expanses, whereas the latter are far more wooded. The Chilterns, however, do become more open in their most easterly stretches in the area of the Dunstable Downs.

There are some obvious similarities between the Chilterns and the Cotswolds, their limestone counterparts some 40 miles to the west. Both ranges are partially bordered by the Thames, both are aligned on a roughly south-west/

The Thames at Goring Lock

north-east axis, both have a steep western escarpment, and conversely in both cases their rivers mainly drain south-eastwards, flowing through a series of gentle valleys and eventually into the Thames.

Punctuating the western escarpment of the Chilterns is a succession of fine viewpoints – Watlington Hill, Chinnor Hill, Ivinghoe Beacon and Coombe Hill – overlooking the clay lowlands of the Oxford Plain, Vale of Aylesbury and Bedfordshire. The highest of these, Coombe Hill, is (852ft/260m), a magnificent vantage point owned and preserved by the National Trust and crowned by a monument to the Boer War.

Because of its combination of scenery and solitude, allied with easy access to London, this area has long been popular with political leaders and other eminent figures. Chequers, visible from Coombe Hill, has been the official country residence of British prime ministers since it was given to the nation for that purpose in 1921. Benjamin Disraeli lived at Hughenden Manor near High Wycombe and is buried in the churchyard there.

Herbert Asquith and the writer George Orwell are buried at Sutton Courtenay near Abingdon and W.H. Smith, founder of the books and stationery empire, is buried at Hambleden. The 19th-century Prime Minister Lord John Russell is buried in the Russell family vault in the church at Chenies in the Chess valley, and Clement Attlee lived at Prestwood near Great Missenden.

Many would claim that the chief glory of the Chilterns is the beech woods that extend over much of the area, and indeed it is these that gave rise to the traditional furniture industry of High Wycombe, Chesham and other towns in the area. Walking through these woods is always sheer delight, but inevitably they look best when clothed in autumnal tints of russet and gold. The white arrows painted on tree trunks to indicate the line of the many public footpaths that thread their way through these woods are invaluable and make for generally trouble-free walking.

Another attractive feature of the Chilterns is their many dry valleys, which also provide pleasant walking. In fact rivers are something of a rarity and are generally little more than streams. Two exceptions are the rivers Misbourne and Chess, which both flow through attractive valleys. Cultivated farmland, managed woodland, small manor houses, picturesque villages, pleasant market towns and imposing stately homes have been added to this natural beauty over the centuries to create a neat, orderly landscape, doubly valuable for being so near London.

South of the Chilterns the Thames flows through a broad, undulating valley, bordered by Oxfordshire, Berkshire and Buckinghamshire, before continuing through London and on to its estuary. This is a different terrain and a different kind of walking. For most of the river's length public footpaths line at least one bank – in some areas both banks – at times crossing flat meadows with wide vistas and at other times proceeding either through or below fine wooded stretches. A series of historic towns and delightful riverside villages add to the pleasures of walking by the Thames, and a succession of viewpoints above the valley – Wittenham Clumps, Winter Hill, Cooper's Hill – give superb views over the winding river. Perhaps the most spectacular views are those on either side of the Goring Gap, where the valley narrows as the Thames cuts through the gap between the Chilterns and the Berkshire Downs.

Throughout the centuries proximity to London has ensured that this area has always been in the mainstream of English history and has played a vital role in the nation's communications network. Probably the oldest routeway in the country, known as the Ridgeway to the west of the Thames and the Icknield Way to the east, follows the line of the chalk ridge across the region, part of a prehistoric trackway from Dorset to Norfolk. Much of this route now enjoys

Typical Chilterns landscape near Bledlow

a new lease of life as the Ridgeway National Trail.

The Thames itself has always been one of the chief arteries of English history and many important events have taken place near its banks. Windsor Castle, the oldest continuous royal residence and main centre of royal power for over nine centuries, rises majestically above it. On the opposite bank stands Eton, the country's most prestigious public school. A few miles downstream, on Runnymede Meadows, King John was forced to sign Magna Carta in 1215, and a little further downstream is Hampton Court Palace, the nearest England has to a Versailles. Beyond that are the fragmentary remains of Richmond Palace, built by the founder of the Tudor dynasty Henry VII, and where that same dynasty came to an end with the death of Elizabeth I in 1603.

The towns that line the Thames mainly grew up at important bridging points. Despite increased traffic, suburban expansion and the establishment of new hi-tech industries around their fringes, most of them have managed to preserve their individuality and attractive qualities. Abingdon and Wallingford are two good examples. Although they have both lost their major outstanding medieval buildings – only fragments survive of Abingdon Abbey and Wallingford Castle – they still retain a historic 'feel' and possess some fine old buildings, as well as impressive bridges and attractive riverside locations. Marlow and Henley grew up later, as fashionable Georgian and Victorian riverside resorts and desirable residential towns, and much of their genteel atmosphere survives. Dorchester, standing near the confluence of the Thames and Thame, was once the major ecclesiastical centre of the region. Now it is a sleepy but appealing backwater, with only part of the church surviving from its large medieval abbey. Windsor of course still retains its greatest asset, the magnificent royal castle, containing buildings from the 11th to the 19th centuries, the major tourist attraction of the region.

Whereas the principal towns of the Thames Valley grew up at crossing-points over the river, the main Chiltern towns – High Wycombe, Princes Risborough, Amersham and most recent Berkhamsted – were established at strategic gaps in the hills which became major routeways between London and the Midlands and North of England. Early roads and tracks through these gaps were successively upgraded and added to over the centuries. The 18th century produced canals, the 19th and early 20th centuries brought the railways, the late 20th century introduced motorways, and the most recent development is the planned route of HS2. Berkhamsted is a particularly interesting town in which to observe these changes; here the remains of the 11th-century Norman castle (itself a recognition of the strategic importance of the site) overlook the A41, the Grand Union Canal and main railway line from London to the Midlands, North West and Scotland.

One quality of the region that is likely to make itself quickly apparent to any walker is that despite the main roads, motorways and railways, despite the proximity of Heathrow airport and the seemingly inexorable spread of suburban London, many parts still manage to preserve an air of peace and tranquillity that gives the impression that they are genuinely off the beaten track. This is more true of the Chilterns than the Thames Valley; in the latter area there always appears to be plenty of activity and traffic, albeit of the leisure variety, on the river. But in areas of the Chilterns there are a number of delightful and largely unchanged villages – like Hambleden, Turville, Fingest, Bradenham, Bledlow, Sarratt and Aldbury – and lonely valleys and silent beech woods that could be both remote in distance from London and far in time from the 21st century.

'Civilised' is perhaps an appropriate adjective to describe walking in the Thames Valley and Chilterns. The landscape is pleasant and gentle rather than dramatic, intimate rather than challenging, a landscape of rolling wooded hills and arable fields, open commons and sheltered valleys, largely tamed over the centuries. Given the obvious commercial, transport and population pressures in this part of England, it is a landscape that has survived remarkably intact and unspoilt.

There is plenty of varied walking in the area, with mainly flat or gently undulating rambles by the Thames contrasting with more energetic walks in the hills. Waymarking is of a high standard, among the best in the country, and although some muddy and overgrown stretches of path can be found in the remoter and less frequently walked areas, paths, stiles and footbridges are generally in a good condition. Much of the credit for this must go to the active and ever-watchful Chiltern Society. Two national trails, the Ridgeway and the Thames Path, pass through the area and most of the county councils in the region have devised short and middle-distance routes and circular walks which, like the national trails, benefit from good waymarking.

Put on your boots and rucksack, pick up a map or guidebook and you will realise that in this highly vulnerable area of the Home Counties, you can still quickly escape into a world of peace and solitude, of quiet and unspoilt country, that perhaps you felt was only attainable in the more remote and sparsely populated parts of England. Long may this state of affairs continue.

This book includes a list of waypoints alongside the description of the walk, so that you can enjoy the full benefits of GPS should you wish to. For more information on using your GPS, read the Pathfinder® Guide *GPS for Walkers*, by GPS teacher and navigation trainer, Clive Thomas (ISBN 978-0-7117-4445-5). For essential information on map reading and basic navigation, read the Pathfinder® Guide *Map Reading Skills* by outdoor writer, Terry Marsh (ISBN 978-0-7117-4978-8). Both titles are available in bookshops or can be ordered online at www.crimsonpublishing.co.uk

Padworth Mill
at Aldermaston

Wallingford

Start
Wallingford, on the east side of the bridge

Distance
2½ miles (4km)

Height gain
80 feet (25m)

Approximate time
1½ hours

Route terrain
Field and riverside paths

Parking
Riverside Park car park

OS maps
Landranger 175 (Reading & Windsor), Explorer 171 (Chiltern Hills West)

GPS waypoints
✐ SU 611 894
Ⓐ SU 612 893
Ⓑ SU 616 880
Ⓒ SU 610 880

Attractive riverside scenery and the chance to explore the interesting old town of Wallingford are the main features of this easy walk along field and tree-lined paths, finishing with a pleasant half-mile stroll by the banks of the Thames.

Wallingford

Wallingford is an ancient town and one of the few in England that still possesses its Saxon earth defences. These were constructed around three sides of the town; the fourth side was protected by the Thames. Of the castle – built in the late 11th century by William the Conqueror to guard this important river crossing, and one of the largest in the country – only a few crumbling walls remain, but the site is an attractive one, now a public park, with fine views over the Thames Valley. Despite being destroyed by the Danes in 1006, decimated by the Black Death in 1349 and devastated by fire in 1675, Wallingford retains an air of antiquity. Its surviving churches, a 17th century town hall and some fine Georgian houses, along with the Saxon ramparts and Norman castle site, all testify to its former greatness.

 From the car park turn left to head up to the road, continue along it and just before the entrance to a camp and caravan site and the village sign for Crowmarsh Gifford, turn right along a tree-lined track Ⓐ. At a fork just in front of a metal gate take the left-hand tree-lined path, which later emerges into more open country and continues across fields between wire fences.

At a T-junction turn right for a few paces along a tarmac track and then turn sharp left through a kissing-gate to follow a path straight across a field. Maintain the same direction in the next field, climb a stile and on reaching the road at the top of steps, cross over to a public footpath sign and a plank bridge Ⓑ. Follow the path through the trees and turn right to join the Ridgeway. Walk along a tree-lined path with the A4130 close by on the right. Go through a wrought iron gate to reach a junction of paths just to the left of a new footpath underpass Ⓒ.

Turn right, pass under the road and continue along a paved path. Where this bears right through a gate, keep ahead along a tree-lined path, passing to the left of school buildings. On reaching a farm, climb a stile to the left of a house and continue along a track, between farm buildings on the left and a house on the right. Go through a kissing-gate and keep ahead

Wallingford

SCALE 1:25000 or 2½ INCHES to 1 MILE 4CM to 1KM

along the right-hand edge of a meadow by a wire fence on the right. After about 50 yds turn left by a waymarked post and head straight across the meadow – there is no visible path – to the river. Turn right and follow the Thames back to Wallingford Bridge, enjoying attractive views of the houses of Wallingford on the opposite bank. Pass under the bridge and turn right to return to the car park. ●

walk 2

Watlington Hill

Start	Watlington Hill
Distance	2¾ miles (4.4km)
Height gain	345 feet (105m)
Approximate time	1½ hours
Route terrain	Downland tracks and field paths
Parking	National Trust car park at Watlington Hill
OS maps	Landranger 175 (Reading & Windsor), Explorer 171 (Chiltern Hills West)

GPS waypoints

- SU 709 935
- Ⓐ SU 713 934
- Ⓑ SU 700 928
- Ⓒ SU 714 929

From the car park at Watlington Hill, one of the high points on the Chiltern escarpment and a superb viewpoint overlooking the clay lowlands of the Oxfordshire Plain, this spectacular walk skirts Lower Deans Wood before climbing steeply to another superb vantage point. The walk then passes within sight of imposing Watlington Park, a privately owned house, before cutting through glorious beech woodland to reach the charmingly named hamlet of Christmas Common.

Watlington Hill

Watlington Hill was given to the National Trust in 1941 by the 3rd Viscount and Viscountess Esher. The hill consists of a large area of chalk down and copse rising to over 700 ft on the north escarpment of the Chilterns. On the lower slopes of the hill the outline of a church steeple is visible, carved into the chalk. The carving is best seen from a distance and is intended to give the impression that the church in Watlington, just below the hill, has a spire when viewed from the Oxfordshire Plain.

Begin by making for the road and turn right towards Christmas Common. Follow the road and about 100yds before a junction turn right at a footpath sign Ⓐ to go through a gate. Bear right for a few paces to two gates. Take the left gate and follow the enclosed path with the cooling towers of Didcot Power Station seen on the horizon. Follow the path between trees and banks of vegetation. Farther on there are fields and stretches of downland on the right. Along here you may catch sight of deer grazing among the trees and open pasture. Continue for some time along the perimeter of Lower Deans Wood and look for occasional white arrows. Join a track at Lower Dean, pass a barn conversion and the old farmhouse and continue along the access track to another house. Beyond it turn left at the intersection Ⓑ and after a few paces, as the track bends right, go through a gate and straight on uphill, climbing steeply. Head towards trees and pause to glance back for lovely views to the west. Enter the woodland and turn left after several paces. Follow the path through a break in the trees and on the right is a striking view of Watlington Park. Continue through the woods, at one point bend right and keep ahead until eventually you reach a drive. Turn left to the road Ⓒ and then left again to pass the former church of the Nativity, dating back to 1889, on the right and then an historic 500-year-old

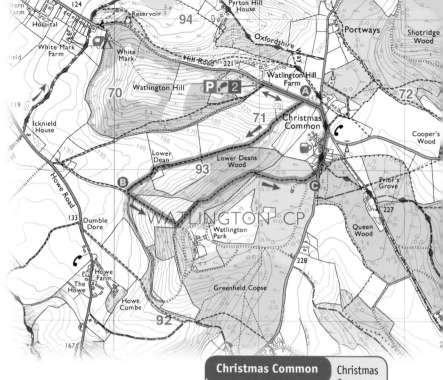

SCALE 1:25000 or 2½ INCHES to 1 MILE 4CM to 1KM

0   200   400   600   800 METRES   1
|___|___|___|___|___| KILOMETRES
0   200   400   600 YARDS   ½   MILES

pub, the **Fox and Hounds**, on the left. Continue through Christmas Common, pass a turning to North End on the right and take the next left turn (Watlington). Pass the speed de-restriction sign and follow the road back to the car park at Watlington Hill.

Christmas Common

Christmas Common apparently takes its name from an extraordinary incident here during the Civil War. In the Christmas of 1643 the Parliamentarians held nearby Watlington while the Royalists defended the ridge on which this hamlet is situated. Because it was Christmas a temporary truce was called and both armies met on this spot during the festivities.

Watlington Hill

WATLINGTON HILL ● 13

walk 3

Start

Burnham Beeches, on corner of A355 and Harehatch Lane, 1 mile (1.6km) north of Farnham Common

Distance

3½ miles (5.5km)

Height gain

165 feet (50m)

Approximate time

1½ hours

Route terrain

Woodland tracks, lanes

Parking

Small parking area at start. Alternatively, roadside parking at Hedgerley Hill just south of Ⓑ

OS maps

Landranger 175 (Reading & Windsor), Explorer 172 (Chiltern Hills East)

GPS waypoints

SU 954 870
Ⓐ SU 968 871
Ⓑ SU 968 867
Ⓒ SU 959 866
Ⓓ SU 956 862
Ⓔ SU 946 864

Hedgerley and Burnham Beeches

Burnham Beeches, a large expanse of natural and unspoilt woodland lying between Beaconsfield and Slough, was bought by the Corporation of the City of London in 1879 to be preserved for public enjoyment and recreation. It is renowned for its many gnarled, ancient trees. After heading across farmland and along a lane to the village of Hedgerley, the walk continues mostly through the northern part of this attractive and popular area. Almost the whole route is well-waymarked with Buckinghamshire County Council 'Circular Walk' signs.

Begin by crossing the A355 and taking the tarmac drive opposite to Pennlands Farm. Follow the drive – mostly tree-lined – down to the farm, pass to the right of it and continue along the track ahead, between a wire fence on the left and a hedge on the right, to meet a lane junction.

Keep straight ahead along narrow Kiln Lane, passing in front of a row of cottages, for just under ¹/₂ mile to a T-junction in the pleasant and secluded village of Hedgerley Ⓐ. The main part of the village and the rebuilt 19th-century church are to the left, but the route continues to the right along a road for ¹/₄ mile, heading uphill between trees. After passing Gregory Road on the right turn right Ⓑ, at a half-hidden public footpath sign, along a tarmac path between garden fences and hedges.

If parking at Hedgerley Hill a little further on along the road, you join the walk at this public footpath sign.

Cross a road and continue along the path opposite, also between fences, passing through a wooden barrier to a junction of paths on the edge of woodland. Keep ahead, in the direction of a Circular Walk waymarked post, along a woodland path; at a fork ahead continue along the left-hand path. At another fork follow the direction of a waymark to take the left-hand path again and follow the regular waymarks through the wood to climb a stile and continue to a road. Turn right, keep ahead at a crossroads and, ¹/₄ mile farther on, turn left Ⓒ at a waymarked path into woodland. Walk through the wood, by a fence on the left, and climb a stile on to the A355 again. Cross the road, to a narrow path opposite and continue between fences through a lovely area of woodland to reach another lane Ⓓ.

Cross the lane, go through a white gate to enter Burnham

In Egypt Woods, Burnham Beeches

Beeches and walk along a concrete drive. Pass in front of houses and continue along the path ahead through Egypt Woods, the northern part of Burnham Beeches and named after a former gypsy encampment. The path heads downhill to a fork at the bottom. Here take the left-hand path – the waymarked post is almost obscured by bracken – to continue gently uphill to a T-junction of paths on the edge of woodland **E**. At this point follow the Circular Walk sign sharply to the right along a path that keeps along the left-hand edge of woodland, by a wire fence on the left, then continues once more through the trees.

Follow this well-waymarked path for ½ mile, eventually climbing a stile and keeping ahead to go over another one on to the lane at the starting point. ●

SCALE 1:25000 or 2½ INCHES to 1 MILE 4CM to 1KM

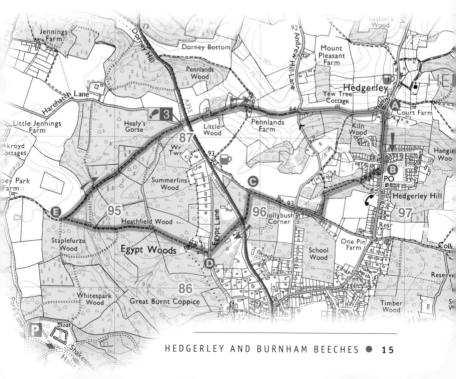

West Woodhay and Inkpen

Start

West Woodhay at St Laurence's Church

Distance

3½ miles (5.4km)

Height gain

165 feet (50m)

Approximate time

1½ hours

Route terrain

Lanes, tracks and field paths

P Parking

Limited roadside parking in the vicinity of the church

OS maps

Landranger 174 (Newbury & Wantage), Explorer 158 (Newbury & Hungerford)

GPS waypoints

SU 390 630
Ⓐ SU 384 633
Ⓑ SU 375 633
Ⓒ SU 389 623

Close to the start of this delightful walk are good views of West Woodhay House, built by Inigo Jones for Sir Benjamin Rudyard, a poet and eminent politician. Rudyard sat for 24 years in Parliament and his renowned sense of justice forced him to take a stand against the king during the Civil War. Following his appeal for peace, Rudyard was expelled from Parliament and retired to West Woodhay, where he died in 1658. From the house the walk cuts across country to a welcome pub and then returns to West Woodhay against a spectacular backdrop of green hills and dramatic downland straddling the Berkshire/ Hampshire border.

St Laurence's Church

St Laurence's Church was built in 1883 in the style of Early English Revival and incorporating local flint and Bath stone in its construction. The present church replaces two previous ones and a number of relics from the earlier churches still remain – among them some tiles which are preserved in the bell tower. The church includes several memorials to the Cole family who lived at West Woodhay until the early 20th century. The estate subsequently passed to the Henderson family and the delightful garden adjacent to the churchyard was established by Johnny Henderson in memory of his wife Sarah who was killed in a riding accident in 1972.

With your back to St Laurence's Church turn right along the road, look for West Woodhay House with a lake visible below it and ignore a turning for Kintbury on the right. Follow the road round a left bend, passing farm outbuildings, and take the next track on the right Ⓐ. Follow the restricted byway, with Combe Gibbet seen on the south-westerly horizon, and pass some brick and tile-hung cottages. Keep to the track, ascend through trees and over to the right is an isolated house. Pass over a path junction and at the next road turn left opposite Thornton Cottage. Walk beside the **Crown and Garter** pub, keep left at the fork, towards Combe and Faccombe, and farther on follow the road down through trees. Head for the next road junction Ⓑ and turn left. Pass Kirby House on the right and begin climbing the hill. Just beyond a thatched cottage turn left at a footpath sign and climb the bank. Branch left in the field and keep alongside the boundary. Head for a waymark at the end of the trees and hedge and continue out across the field. At the road, on the far side, turn right and pass some paddocks on the left. Look for the village sign for West Woodhay and when the road bends right by Park House, keep ahead at the footpath sign. Follow the grassy track as it bends left, passing between fields. The ridge of Combe Hill and Walbury Hill is seen to the south. Make for a curtain of woodland and follow the track to the right of it, soon swinging left. Keep the trees on the left and climb the slope to high ground. Bear left, then right and follow the track to farm outbuildings. At a concrete track, by a bridleway sign ⓒ, turn left and walk along to the road. Turn left, then left again at the next junction, returning to St Laurence's Church. ●

West Woodhay church

Combe Gibbet

Combe Gibbet was first erected in 1676 so that a local man, George Broomham, and his mistress, Dorothy Newman, could be hanged for the brutal murder of Broomham's wife and son. It was never used again, though there has been a gibbet on this site ever since. The story became the subject of a film, The Black Legend, made in 1948, directed by John Schlesinger and starring a young Robert Hardy as Mad Thomas. Many roles were played by locals.

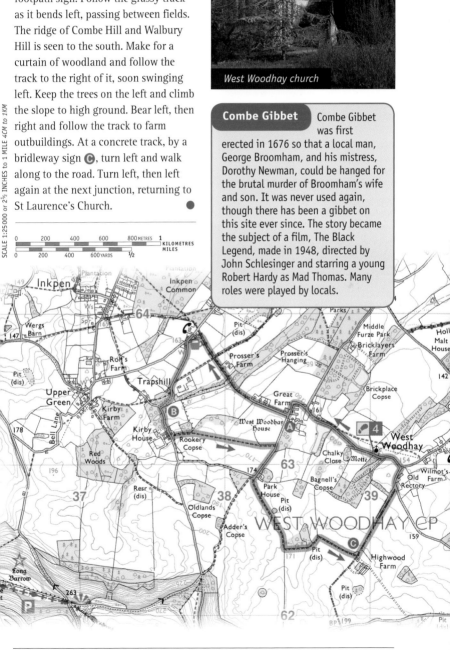

Dorchester and Wittenham Clumps

Start
Dorchester

Distance
4 miles (6.5km)

Height gain
310 feet (95m)

Approximate time
2 hours

Route terrain
Thames Path and field, downland and woodland paths

Parking
Bridge End car park at start

OS maps
Landranger 164 (Oxford) or 174 (Newbury & Wantage), Explorer 170 (Abingdon, Wantage & Vale of White Horse)

GPS waypoints
SU 578 939
Ⓐ SU 577 936
Ⓑ SU 568 934
Ⓒ SU 566 933
Ⓓ SU 566 927
Ⓔ SU 569 924

An attractive village, an ancient abbey, riverside meadows, an Iron Age settlement, a medieval church, a prehistoric hillfort and fine woodland all feature in a remarkably varied walk for such a modest distance. The steep but short climb to Wittenham Clumps is rewarded with one of the finest views over the Thames Valley.

Dorchester Before the Norman Conquest, Dorchester was a cathedral city, headquarters of the largest diocese in England, but the Normans transferred the see to Lincoln. On the site of the Saxon cathedral an Augustinian abbey was founded and the church, noted for its Norman nave and fine 13th and 14th-century choir, largely survived the Dissolution of the monasteries, although the rest of the monastic buildings were destroyed. Later Dorchester became an important staging post on the London–Oxford road – hence the large coaching inns in High Street – but is now a sleepy, attractive backwater.

The walk starts at the southern end of High Street near the more southerly of the two entrances to the abbey grounds. Follow Bridge End and, just after passing the Catholic church on the left, bear right, at a public footpath sign to 'River and Wittenham', along a stony track – Wittenham Lane – between some picturesque cottages. After the last cottage continue along the field edge path bending right to a kissing-gate Ⓐ. Keep ahead beyond it. On your right are the Dyke Hills, the ramparts of an Iron Age settlement that augmented the natural defences provided by the rivers Thame and Thames. Beyond the pillbox the path curves a little to the left on to the field terrace. Look ahead for another kissing-gate through a fence, beyond which you reach the bank of the Thames just above its confluence with the Thame. Turn right alongside the Thames, pass through two gates and eventually follow it around a right-hand bend to Little Wittenham Bridge Ⓑ.

Go through a gate to pass under the bridge, turn right and then right again, go through another gate and cross Little Wittenham Bridge, actually three bridges in succession over different channels of the Thames. Continue along a tarmac path to Little Wittenham church and opposite it turn left through a gate into Little Wittenham Nature Reserve Ⓒ.

Ahead is a fork; take the right-hand path which continues along the right-hand edge of a meadow, by a hedge on the right, making directly for Wittenham Clumps, part of the Sinodun Hills which rise abruptly above the surrounding flat terrain. Go through a gate and head steeply uphill across the open grassy hillside to Round Hill, the prominent tree circle in front **D**. The steep climb is rewarded with a magnificent view of the Thames Valley, the river below and Dorchester Abbey clearly visible.

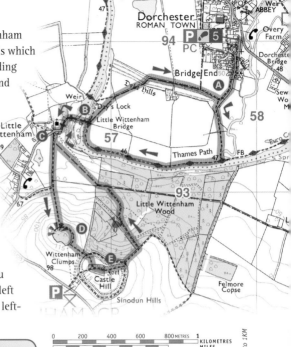

With your back to the trees, turn right and follow the Clumps' perimeter path until you are level with Castle Hill on the left and a seat on the right. Take the left-hand path here.

> ### Castle Hill
> Consists of an Iron Age fort, comprising circular ramparts and ditch. There is evidence that the fort continued to be occupied after the Roman conquest and might even have been used by the Saxons.

Cross a track, continue to a gate and at a fork ahead bear right to head up through the outer defences of the fort. Walk across the grass to enter the trees which crown the fort, and by a waymarked post keep ahead to a T-junction of paths. Turn left to continue through the impressive woodland that crowns Castle Hill.

On emerging from the trees **E** go diagonally down the grassy slopes, dropping down an embankment to turn left through a galvanised gate. Continue downhill along the left-hand edge of a field, bordered by woods on the left, and go through a gate on the left about two-thirds of the way down. Follow the downhill path ahead along the right-hand side of a grassy ride through Little Wittenham Wood, and at the bottom

bear slightly left on to a wide uphill track. Near the top, bear right on to a path running through the trees and on reaching a junction with a clear path, keep left to a gate, turn half-right and head diagonally over a meadow to join the previous route in the far corner **C**, just in front of a gate.

Retrace your steps to Little Wittenham Bridge and after crossing the third and last of the succession of bridges **B**, go through a gate and turn half-left to follow a faint but discernible path across a meadow, heading in the direction of the tower of Dorchester Abbey. Go through another gate and continue along a hedge- and fence-lined path which passes through the Dyke Hills and then bears right to continue alongside them. Cross a track, keep along the right-hand edge of a field – still beside the 'dykes' on the right – and in the field corner turn left **A**, here rejoining the outward route again to retrace your steps to the start. ●

✏ Start
Aldermaston Wharf

⚑ Distance
4 miles (6.5km)

⛰ Height gain
Negligible

⏱ Approximate time
2 hours

👢 Route terrain
Canal towpath, lane, field paths and tracks

P Parking
Visitor centre car park at Aldermaston Wharf, signposted off the A4 to the west of the M4 junction 12 at Theale. Alternative car park at Aldermaston Station nearby

🗺 OS maps
Landranger 174 (Newbury & Wantage) and 175 (Reading & Windsor), Explorer 159 (Reading)

📷 GPS waypoints
✏ SU 603 671
Ⓐ SU 590 666
Ⓑ SU 592 661
Ⓒ SU 594 655
Ⓓ SU 606 664

Aldermaston and the Kennet & Avon Canal

Only by exploring on foot can you discover a network of delightfully hidden paths and tracks threading their way through the Kennet valley between Aldermaston Wharf and Aldermaston village. The latter includes a picturesque street of handsome houses and quaint cottages, while the former illustrates the Kennet & Avon Canal's long and eventful history. The walk in between is delightfully quiet and leafy.

✏ From the visitor centre turn right to the lift bridge at Aldermaston Wharf. Cross to the southern bank of the canal and follow the towpath west. Beyond Aldermaston Lock the path passes between trees and banks of thick foliage. Continue all the way to the next road Ⓐ and turn left. Pass Fronds Farm and follow the road to the next junction. Turn right here and pass the entrance to the Old Mill Hotel, once a flour mill. Cross the road at the bridge just beyond the entrance and once across turn left to enter a copse of poplar trees Ⓑ. Follow the path down the bank, emerge from the trees at a wooden footbridge and take the path across three fields to a galvanised gate Ⓒ in the hedge.

Turn right and walk along Fisherman's Lane to visit Aldermaston village, then retrace your steps along the track. Over on the right there are glimpses of Aldermaston's Church of St Mary the Virgin, its tower peeping between the trees. The church contains some medieval wall paintings and an alabaster figure of Sir George Forster, a distinguished soldier who lived in the nearby manor house during the reign of Henry VIII.

Pass the footpath from the Old Mill Hotel on the left and on the right is a path leading up to Aldermaston church. Pass a brick cottage with weeping willows in the garden and continue along the track. Follow it alongside trees to a kissing-gate by a small parking area and keep ahead, eventually reaching a second gate. Cross into the field and keep the boundary on your left. Make for the far corner of the pasture and take the footbridge into the next field. Keep ahead and look to the right for a brief glimpse of 18th century Padworth House on the hillside. The parkland is thought to have been designed by Capability Brown. Over halfway across the field look for a footpath sign and a junction of rights of way.

The Kennet & Avon Canal

The Kennet & Avon Canal has had a chequered history but is without doubt one of the great engineering triumphs of the early 19th century. The 87-mile canal dates back to 1810 and was originally built as a trade route to link Reading and Bristol. Timber and coal were among many products conveyed along this vital inland waterway which made its debut late in the canal era. The railway era eventually killed it off and it closed to navigation in 1951. For years it lay derelict and abandoned. Thanks to dedicated supporters and enthusiasts, however, this most famous of inland waterways was restored and revived. The Queen reopened the Kennet & Avon in 1990. Today it draws visitors from far and wide – boaters steer their craft along its meandering route and walkers, anglers and cyclists return time and again to savour its beauty and tranquility.

Turn left ❹, cross a wooden footbridge over a stream and go straight across the field to a gate. Cross the Kennet by the sluice gates and follow the path alongside some wooden panel fencing to reach Padworth Mill, originally a flour mill. Keep ahead beside more fencing and lines of evergreens to reach a junction with a track. Turn left, pass beneath some horse chestnut trees and follow the lane alongside a row of brick and tile-hung cottages dating back to 1876. Continue to Alder Bridge School and at the junction turn right. Cross the lift bridge, then turn right and return to the visitor centre and the car park. ●

SCALE 1:25000 or 2½ INCHES to 1 MILE 4CM to 1KM

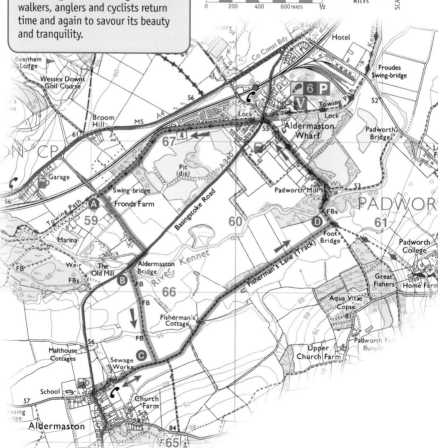

walk 7

Start
Cuckhamsley Hill

Distance
4½ miles (7km)

Height gain
195 feet (60m)

Approximate time
2 hours

Route terrain
Downland tracks

Parking
Lane end car park at Cuckhamsley Hill, 2½ miles (4km) south of East Hendred

OS maps
Landranger 174 (Newbury & Wantage), Explorer 170 (Abingdon, Wantage & Vale of White Horse)

GPS waypoints
- SU 457 850
- Ⓐ SU 451 833
- Ⓑ SU 447 832
- Ⓒ SU 433 846

Cuckhamsley Hill and the Ridgeway

Crossed by the Ridgeway, Cuckhamsley Hill rises to a height of 666ft (203m) above the downs near the border between Oxfordshire and Berkshire. This short walk explores an area of remote, virtually uninhabited countryside characterised by wide and sweeping vistas; the openness of the downs here to the west of the Thames Valley is in striking contrast to the more wooded Chilterns to the east.

At the car park entrance turn right along a track, in the 'Public Right Of Way' direction shown on a footpath sign, across the downs. Immediately there are striking and expansive views, with the Thames Valley away in the distance on the left. The track gently descends and bears gradually right to reach a road Ⓐ.

Turn right along the road for ¹⁄₄ mile, and just in front of a solitary house turn right Ⓑ on to a track – there is a public

Open downland near Cuckhamsley Hill

bridleway sign ahead. At a fork take the left-hand grassy track – a blue waymark and plenty of white arrows indicate the correct route – and follow it for 1¼ miles, through a shallow valley and then climbing gently through woodland up to the ridge ahead. Turn right **C** to join the Ridgeway and follow it for 1½ miles back to the start.

This is a fine scenic section with extensive views from both sides across what appears to be remote and uninhabited country, although later, Didcot power station and Harwell Laboratory are visible reminders of the 21st century. For the last ¼ mile the route passes between trees; Scutchamer Knob, a Saxon burial mound, is situated in the woodland on the right beside the car park. ●

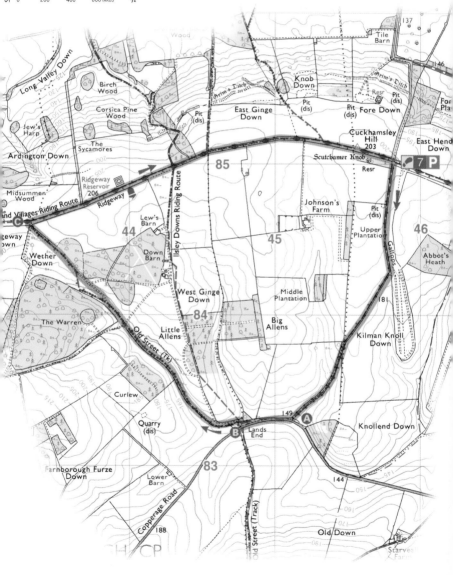

walk 8

Port Meadow

Start	Wolvercote
Distance	4½ miles (7km)
Height gain	Negligible
Approximate time	2 hours
Route terrain	Lane, Thames Path and open meadow
Parking	Public car park at Lower Wolvercote
OS maps	Landranger 164 (Oxford), Explorer 180 (Oxford)

GPS waypoints

- SP 487 094
- Ⓐ SP 491 097
- Ⓑ SP 495 086
- Ⓒ SP 496 076
- Ⓓ SP 483 092

The city of Oxford boasts many splendours – not least among them is Port Meadow, the key feature of this very pleasant undemanding walk in the shadow of the world-famous colleges. Covering 345 acres, the ancient common is where the Freemen and Commoners of Oxford can graze cattle, geese and horses. This charming tradition is even referred to in the Domesday survey of 1086. Port Meadow is the perfect green lung for city dwellers and visitors alike, alive with history and imbued with a wonderful sense of space and tranquility.

From the car park entrance keep right and walk between the houses of Lower Wolvercote, passing two adjoining pubs, the **Red Lion** and the **White Hart**. Pass Home Close and Rowland Close, then the village post office. Keep ahead to Elmthorpe Road and here turn right Ⓐ on to Wolvercote Common and Port Meadow.

Follow the clear path towards the railway embankment and just before reaching it, bear right to follow a grassy path which curves away from the line to reach a cobbled bridge over a ditch. Maintain the same direction, avoid a gate which soon comes into view on the left and continue towards the right edge of a headland of trees. As you approach them look for a footbridge and a kissing-gate. Cross the grass to the gate Ⓑ and continue for a few paces to a path on a bend. Keep right here and follow the path just inside the trees, with glimpses between them of the vast grassy expanse of Port Meadow. Bear right at a junction with a track and follow it through Burgess Field Nature Park. Return to the open ground of Port Meadow and head south towards a car park. Turn right just before it at a kissing-gate and follow the bridleway to a broad footbridge spanning the Thames – or Isis.

Over the bridge turn right to a second footbridge and then cross to the opposite bank, heading upstream by Bossom's Boatyard and Medley Sailing Club. Keep on the Thames Path and along this stretch is a turning to **The Perch** at Binsey Ⓒ, a famous pub in this part of Oxford. CS Lewis often walked this section of the towpath and would invariably stop for a drink at The Perch. Lewis Carroll's *Alice's Adventures in Wonderland*, published in 1865, was inspired by a boat trip Carroll made along this stretch of the river in the summer of 1862. The main walk continues by the Thames and before long reaches the ruins of Godstow Lock.

Pass beside them and make for a gate leading out to the road **D**. Turn right and cross the bridge over the Thames by the **Trout Inn**. Colin Dexter describes this ancient 12th century pub as a 'fine riverside hostelry ' in his Inspector Morse novel *The Jewel that was Ours*. Follow the road back to the car park. ●

The Thames or Isis at Wolvercote

SCALE 1:25000 or 2½ INCHES to 1 MILE 4CM to 1KM

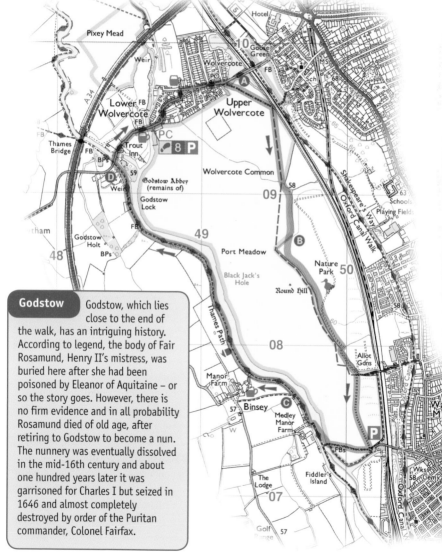

Godstow Godstow, which lies close to the end of the walk, has an intriguing history. According to legend, the body of Fair Rosamund, Henry II's mistress, was buried here after she had been poisoned by Eleanor of Aquitaine – or so the story goes. However, there is no firm evidence and in all probability Rosamund died of old age, after retiring to Godstow to become a nun. The nunnery was eventually dissolved in the mid-16th century and about one hundred years later it was garrisoned for Charles I but seized in 1646 and almost completely destroyed by order of the Puritan commander, Colonel Fairfax.

Old Boars Hill

Start
Wootton

Distance
4¾ miles (7.7km)

Height gain
410 feet (125m)

Approximate time
2½ hours

Route terrain
Lanes, tracks and field paths

Parking
Car park opposite Wootton church, ¼ mile (400m) north of B4017

OS maps
Landranger 164 (Oxford), Explorer 180 (Oxford)

GPS waypoints
- SP 476 013
- Ⓐ SP 481 015
- Ⓑ SP 485 022
- Ⓒ SP 491 020
- Ⓓ SP 485 034
- Ⓔ SP 483 027

The gentle wooded slopes of Old Boars Hill rise to 540ft (165m) to the south-west of Oxford, and from several vantage points on this undemanding walk there are grand views over the city's 'dreaming spires'. In addition there are some equally fine views over the Thames Valley, Chilterns and Berkshire Downs. Part of the route is across land owned by the Oxford Preservation Trust, set up in 1926 to preserve the city's attractive rural setting.

Turn right out of the car park opposite Wootton church and take the first turning on the right, signposted to Old Boars Hill. Follow the lane around first a right-hand and then a left-hand bend, and opposite a house turn left Ⓐ, at a public footpath sign to Cumnor, along a track towards stables. Pass to the right of the stables, climbing several stiles in quick succession, and continue along the right-hand edge of a field, by a hedge on the right, to turn right over a stile in the field corner. Immediately climb another stile and keep left at the immediate fork, crossing the field to the next stile. Keep the hedge over on the left in the next field and look for a galvanised gate. Take the path up the slope to the next gate and follow a narrow path between gardens that merges with a narrow access track (Orchard Lane), shortly to rejoin the lane. Turn left uphill to reach a T-junction at the top Ⓑ.

Bear right here through a gate to enter Jarn Mound and Wild Garden, owned by the Oxford Preservation Trust and constructed under the orders of Sir Arthur Evans, the famous archaeologist, in the early 1930s. The route continues to the right, but keep ahead and climb steps to the top of Jarn Mound for the view over Oxford, the Chilterns and the Berkshire Downs, which is now unfortunately partially obscured by trees. Retrace your steps to the gate and in front of it turn left along the path that passes to the right of a stone commemorating Sir Arthur Evans, and follow this path through the well-wooded garden as it bears left passing through a fence on to a lane. Turn right along the lane, Ridgeway, and at a junction keep ahead along Berkeley Road. At a kissing-gate by an Oxford Preservation Trust notice and collection box, turn left Ⓒ and then turn right to follow a path across delightful, unimproved meadowland, at first keeping parallel to the lane on the right.

Later the path bears left and passes to the left of a copse, fenced tree and bench. From here there is a fine view of Oxford. Head slightly downhill, making for the left edge of the belt of

SCALE 1:25000 or 2½ INCHES to 1 MILE 4CM to 1KM

trees in front where there is a wooden kissing-gate. Go through it and then turn left along the left-hand edge of a field, by a hedge on the left. Go through a metal gate, keep ahead across the next field and go through a wooden gate. Trace the right-hand edge of the next three fields to reach a galvanised gate leading on to a tarmac drive by a pond. Turn left and when the drive bears right to converted farm outbuildings, go straight along the bridleway, part of Hinksey Heights Nature Trail. Veer left by a wooden fence and as the track swings right, follow the field edge beside a brook.

Climb up beside wooden fencing to a stile. A house is visible over on the left. Continue through the trees, keep along the left edge of a field to merge with a track and follow it between pastures to a T-junction of tracks **D**. Turn left along a tarmac track, which keeps along the left edge of Youlbury Wood, passing to the right of a reservoir. Take the first turning on the left, signposted to Oxford, but almost immediately turn right **E** through a gate into the Elizabeth Daryush Memorial Gardens, another piece of land owned by the Oxford Preservation Trust.

Follow a grassy path between trees and soon you reach a pond and benches. Just beyond the pond keep right at the fork and follow the path down to a stile and gateway. Rejoin the tarmac lane and turn left, heading downhill. Later it becomes a broader lane which continues through Wootton village to return to the starting point of the walk.
●

Marlow and Hurley

Start

Marlow

Distance

5½ miles (8.8km)

Height gain

Negligible

Approximate time

2½ hours

Route terrain

Lanes, farm tracks and Thames Path

Parking

Car parks in Marlow

OS maps

Landranger 175 (Reading & Windsor), Explorer 172 (Chiltern Hills East)

GPS waypoints

SU 851 861
Ⓐ SU 847 861
Ⓑ SU 836 848
Ⓒ SU 838 844
Ⓓ SU 826 837
Ⓔ SU 834 841

Marlow is a hugely attractive town with its own rowing regatta and a history that goes back beyond the 'Domesday Book'; it is a lively, buzzing place and a perfect spot from which to begin this easy walk that heads out across meadows to Temple Lock. Shortly afterwards the walk crosses the river via the Temple Footbridge to make a detour to Hurley before returning to Temple Lock and following an outstandingly beautiful section of the Thames back to Marlow.

Marlow The spacious riverside town of Marlow is situated close to some of the most attractive stretches of the Thames. Views of the town are dominated by the suspension bridge over the river and by the church, both dating from the 19th century, and the town as a whole has a pleasantly old-fashioned Victorian atmosphere.

Start at the north end of the suspension bridge with the church on your right. Walk away from the bridge and turn first left into Pound Lane. Keep ahead at a mini-roundabout adjacent to a car park and take the next left, Lower Pound Lane Ⓐ, a quiet tree-lined lane initially with playing fields on either side. Follow the lane for ½ mile to Pens Place and soon afterwards, beyond a gate and stile, continue ahead along a farm track with an enormous field to the right, eventually reaching a junction of tracks Ⓑ just left of Low Grounds Farm. Branch left and around the left-hand bend follow the track across fields to reach the river Ⓒ.

Turn right and follow the Thames past Temple Lock and up to Temple Footbridge, opened in 1989 on the site of the former Temple Ferry. Turn left over the bridge and turn right to continue along a shady path on the south bank of the river. Pass through a gate at the corner of woodland, continue across meadows and turn right over a footbridge on to Hurley Lock Island. Turn left, walk past the lock, turn left over a similar footbridge, descend steps and follow a tarmac path into the peaceful village of Hurley. The Norman church originally belonged to a small priory and there are a few monastic remains, including a dovecote and tithe barn.

Continue along a road through the village and, just in front of **Ye Olde Bell Inn**, turn left Ⓓ, at a public footpath sign, through a metal kissing-gate to continue along a shady, fence enclosed path. Cross a track and keep ahead by some fencing bordering a caravan site on the left. Climb a stile and continue along a broad track. Where the track bends to the right turn left **E** over a stile, at a public footpath sign, to walk along a pleasant, tree-lined path which leads back to the river. Turn right to retrace your steps over Temple Footbridge to the point where you first joined the river **C**.

Follow the riverside path for nearly $1\frac{1}{2}$ miles back to Marlow, a delightful finale to the walk. Looking over the fields to the left, the Chilterns can be seen and across the river are views of the buildings of Bisham Abbey, a Tudor house on the site of a medieval monastery which is now one of Britain's National Sports Centres, and the beautiful 12th-century Bisham church. Towards the end there are equally fine views ahead of Marlow. By the bridge the riverside path turns left and heads up to the road at the starting point. ●

Across the Thames to Bisham

SCALE 1:25000 or 2½ INCHES to 1 MILE 4CM to 1KM

Widbrook Common and Cliveden Reach

Start
Boulter's Lock, Maidenhead

Distance
5¾ miles (9km)

Height gain
Negligible

Approximate time
2½ hours

Route terrain
Lanes, Thames Path and field paths

Parking
Pay and display car park near Boulter's Lock, about ¾ mile (1.2km) north of Maidenhead Bridge on A4094

OS maps
Landranger 175 (Reading & Windsor), Explorer 172 (Chiltern Hills East)

GPS waypoints
SU 902 825
Ⓐ SU 898 822
Ⓑ SU 892 824
Ⓒ SU 894 852
Ⓓ SU 897 851
Ⓔ SU 907 848

The walk to Cookham is mostly across flat, open meadow and marshland, with fine views across the surrounding countryside. After Cookham the route heads for the Thames and continues along Cliveden Reach, a beautiful stretch of the river below the glorious hanging woods of Cliveden, to return to Boulter's Lock.

Begin by walking away from the main road and take the path that leads from the far left-hand corner of the car park to a road. Turn left to a T-junction, turn right and, just after passing a road called The Pagoda, bear right Ⓐ along a path between fences. Where the path ends, cross a road, continue along the

Looking over the River Thames from Cliveden

road ahead – Summerleaze Road – following it around a left-hand bend. At the junction of Blackamoor Lane and Summerleaze Road **B**, turn right, then immediately left at the sign 'to the Green Way.' Pass between gates and follow the track as it bends right.

Continue between hedges and fences.
When the track bends left, join the
parallel path over a footbridge with a
stream on the right. On reaching some
gates – the entrance to North
Maidenhead Cricket Club – turn right to
cross a footbridge and follow a broad
path. Cross a permitted cycle way and
continue on the Green Way. Join a track
and follow it along the field edge with
hedgerow on the right. Pass a footpath
running off left and after 60yds the
path forks. Keep right, signposted Green
Way East. Bear left at the next sign,
passing between crops on a clear path.
Cliveden House is visible ahead on its
wooded cliff above the Thames and all
around are wide views across flat
meadowland. Pass through a kissing-
gate and then across a footbridge,
keeping parallel to a hedge and trees on
the left to a kissing-gate in the field
corner. Follow the straight path across
farmland and at the end of the field
follow the waymarked footpath to the
right alongside Strand Water. Keep
along the left-hand edge of a second
field and at the end of it cross a track,
bear right to continue between fields by
a metal fence on the left. From here
Cookham church tower is visible on the
left; Cliveden House is ahead.

The route continues along an
enclosed path which emerges on to a
drive at Cookham Moor on the western
edge of the village. Turn right **C** to the
war memorial and continue along High
Street passing a pub – **King's Arms** –
and a café – **Infusions** – to a
T-junction.

At the T-junction turn right, in the
Maidenhead direction, take the first
turning on the left **D** – Mill Lane – and
follow this winding lane for ½ mile. On
reaching some houses bear right, at a
Thames Path sign, along a hedge-lined
path which passes in front of some
garages. Continue along the path which
winds through woodland, keeping
parallel to the lane on the left, to reach
the river **E**.

Turn right to follow the riverside
path along Cliveden Reach, an
exceptionally attractive stretch of the
Thames, for 1½ miles back to Boulter's
Lock. For most of the way the path is
shady and tree-lined. To the right are
extensive views across flat meadows to
the wooded hills on the horizon, and to
the left you pass below the hanging
woods of Cliveden owned by the
National Trust. The path eventually
emerges on to the road opposite the car
park at Boulter's Lock.   ●

Abingdon's famous Town Hall

Goring

Start

Goring

Distance

6½ miles (10.4km)

Height gain

625 feet (190m)

Approximate time

3 hours

Route terrain

Undulating field and woodland paths

Parking

Railway station car park or public car park off the High St (both fee paying)

OS maps

Landranger 174 (Newbury & Wantage) and 175 (Reading & Windsor), Explorer 171 (Chiltern Hills West)

GPS waypoints

SU 602 805
Ⓐ SU 602 808
Ⓑ SU 613 814
Ⓒ SU 625 818
Ⓓ SU 628 812
Ⓔ SU 633 807
Ⓕ SU 632 798
Ⓖ SU 605 806

Based in the south-western fringe of the Chilterns this walk follows an undulating route in an arc to the north, east and south of Goring, passing through a succession of attractive wooded areas. Near the end there are superb views looking across the Thames Valley to the Berkshire Downs.

Leave the station car park passing the station entrance (left) and walk along Gatehampton Road, passing Reading Road (right), and turn left to walk down the High Street to reach the Thames. Take time to absorb the lovely riverside scene from this busy little bridging point.

Goring Goring stands on the eastern bank of the Thames where the river cuts through the Goring Gap between the Chilterns and Berkshire Downs. The bridge linking Goring and Streatley on the western bank dates only from the 19th century; before that it was necessary to cross the river by ferry.

Retrace your steps back through the village turning left out of High Street at the top of the climb and almost immediately turn right down a driveway, signposted Cleeve Ⓐ. Where the drive bends slightly right turn left along a fenced tarmac path to a road. Keep ahead through a modern housing area and where the road ends, continue along a tarmac path for a few paces, then turn right through a fence gap and cross a track.

Follow the waymarked path between fences to a stile, turn right and climb another one after a few paces (Chiltern Way). Follow the grassy path along the lower slopes of a field, with houses visible to the left, and make for another stile in the corner of the pasture. Avoid a stile on the left after a few steps and keep ahead alongside wooden panel fencing. Keep sloping woodland on the right, to emerge on to a lane **B**. Turn right and almost immediately turn left, at a public footpath sign to Beech Lane and Woodcote, along a narrow, enclosed path, later keeping along the left edge of woodland. The path bears right to continue uphill through Wroxhills Wood to a crossroads of paths.

Keep ahead, following the obvious path through the trees. Keep in a fairly straight line, to emerge on to a track in the far corner of the wood. Turn right along this hedge- and tree-lined track and at the point where it becomes a tarmac drive, turn right **C**, at a public footpath sign, along the track

which heads straight across fields and descends to a waymarked stile. Do not climb the stile but turn left and continue gently downhill along a track to go through a metal gate on to a road. Turn left and after about 100 yds bear right **D** along a track through Old Elvendon Wood. Head uphill to emerge from the trees, continue along a track to a road **E**, cross the road and climb a stile opposite, at a public footpath sign. Bear slightly left and follow an obvious path across the field. On the far side pass through a hedge gap to continue between hedgerows. The path curves right and left, following the contours of the field on the right. Soon you re-enter woodland and descend to a track in the valley bottom. Cross this track, take the

SCALE 1:27 777 or 2¼ INCHES to 1 MILE 3.6CM to 1KM

0	200	400	600	800 METRES	1
					KILOMETRES
					MILES
0	200	400	600 YARDS	½	

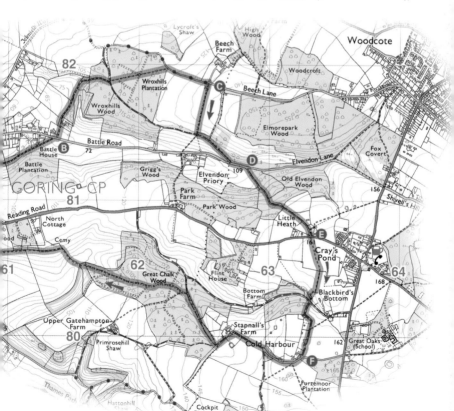

The River Thames at Streatley

uphill path ahead to a house, then turn left along another track in front of the house and follow it as it curves right and continues to a lane **F**.

Turn right along the narrow lane, passing to the left of Coldharbour Farm and follow the lane towards Stapnall's Farm. When you see a sign for Chalkwood House on a tree, bear left to follow the bridleway to a wooden gate into woodland. Pass the remains of another bridlegate and then turn right down a wide path that falls gently through the mainly coniferous Great Chalk Wood. On reaching the waymarked gateway within these woods turn left (do not go through the gateway) and then keep right at the fork. Go straight over the wide crossing trackway and keep left at the nearby fork. At a grassy fork bear right, gradually descending to a waymarked kissing-gate. Go through the gate and continue ahead to the next kissing-gate leading out to an immense field.

Turn right up the field edge, remaining with this round the top corner and ignoring a kissing-gate. There are impressive views from this section.

Pass through the gap at the top of the hedgerow and continue along the head of the next field. At the corner of the pasture turn right and head diagonally across the playing fields to the wooden railing at the end of the line of cupressus **G**. Pass through this into an estate road. Go ahead, turn left, then right at a T-junction to a lane. Turn left to another junction beside **The Queen's Arms** and go left to return to the station or, alternatively, walk right for a few paces to return to the High Street. ●

Whitehorse Hill and Kingston Lisle

walk 13

There is a great deal to commend this spectacular walk in the Vale of White Horse. The views are stunning and the walk is imbued with a strong sense of the past, of ancient history, romantic legends and colourful mythology. Starting on the high ground of Whitehorse Hill, a much-loved beauty spot in the south-west corner of Oxfordshire, the route heads north and then east to the picturesque village of Kingston Lisle, sheltering below the Ridgeway. The return leg involves a breezy, but not unduly strenuous, climb back to Whitehorse Hill.

 From the bottom end of the car park, at a National Trust sign for Whitehorse Hill, go through a gate and follow the path across grassy slopes to a second gate with National Trust signs. Go through the gate and turn left down the narrow lane, passing the National Trust and English Heritage topography map on the left. Continue down the lane, over a cattle-grid and, on reaching the junction, go straight over **Ⓐ** to follow the road towards Uffington.

Pass Sower Hill Farm on the left and ignore a path on the right just beyond Hill Farm House. Continue on the road to the next path on the right (signposted Fawler). Take the path, passing through a galvanised gate. Walk beside woodland to its corner where there is a footpath intersection **Ⓑ**. Keep ahead over the footbridge and straight ahead across the field. Go through a gate on the far side and keep ahead in the grassy pasture. Make for a gate and stile in the hedge and continue ahead in the next field, keeping to the right of the houses of Fawler. Look for a stile in the far boundary and, a few paces beyond it, a gate. Cross a paddock and on the far side go through another gate to cross a footbridge. Head diagonally left across the grass towards some thatched cottages. Pass between them to the road and turn left.

Follow the road out of Fawler and just past the speed de-restriction signs and a village sign, cross a stile on the right **Ⓒ**. Head diagonally across the paddock to the next stile, then forward with fencing on the left towards trees. Look for a stile just to the right of the corner, cross a bridge over a stream and walk ahead in the field, keeping hedgerow on the right. Head for the top right-hand corner, climb a stile and continue up the hillside to the next stile. Follow the grassy track ahead with the

Start
Whitehorse Hill

Distance
6½ miles (10.3km)

Height gain
705 feet (215m)

Approximate time
3 hours

Route terrain
Lanes, downland path and tracks

Ⓟ Parking
National Trust's Uffington Whitehorse and Wayland's Smithy car park on Whitehorse Hill, south of the B4507

OS maps
Landranger 174 (Newbury & Wantage), Explorer 170 (Abingdon, Wantage & Vale of White Horse)

GPS waypoints
SU 293 866
Ⓐ SU 302 872
Ⓑ SU 307 879
Ⓒ SU 318 883
Ⓓ SU 322 878
Ⓔ SU 318 864

The view from Whitehorse Hill

houses of Kingston Lisle looming into view. At the road turn right.

Walk through the village, passing the **Blowing Stone** pub. The church, visible on the left near the junction, includes many Norman and 13th century features and its thick chalk walls are adorned with paintings of the life of St John the Baptist. Keep right at the junction, following the road towards Fawler, Uffington and Faringdon. Pass Kingston Lisle Farm on the left, follow the road as it descends quite steeply and when it curves right, turn left at a footpath sign and stile **D**.

Follow the path ahead across the field towards trees and distant hills. Continue via a stile into the next field, then the next across a stile by a galvanised gate. Go across to a low ladder stile, then keep ahead in the next pasture with hedgerow on your left. Head up the slope to the field corner, go through

a gate and out to the road. Cross over to a footpath sign and gate and go straight ahead along a cinder track.

The cooling towers of Didcot Power Station can be seen way over to the left on the horizon.

Follow the track up to the Ridgeway and turn right **E**. Pass a permissive footpath and stile on the right, a second footpath also on the right and continue as the Ridgeway climbs gently. Keep ahead to a wire fence on the right with a National Trust sign for Whitehorse Hill. Continue on the Ridgeway until you draw level with the ramparts of Uffington Castle and a gate and bridleway sign on the right. Go through the gate and aim towards the trig point ahead. Maintain it on your left and follow the path round the side of the ramparts. Soon it splits. Keep right here, with magnificent views of the Vale of White Horse. Follow the path as it drops down to a narrow access road. Cross to the gate opposite and return to the car park.

The White Horse

The White Horse itself has been scientifically dated to the late Bronze Age, though its origin is unknown. At 365 ft long and 130 ft tall, the splendid galloping figure of the horse is best appreciated from some distance away, or from the air. Also crowning the 850ft-high hill is Uffington Castle, a prehistoric fort covering about 8 acres and roughly oval in shape. The monument is enclosed by ramparts and a deep outer ditch.

SCALE 1:25000 or 2½ INCHES to 1 MILE 4CM to 1KM

| 0 | 200 | 400 | 600 | 800 METRES | 1 |
| 0 | 200 | 400 | 600 YARDS | ½ | KILOMETRES MILES |

walk 14

Start
Cockshoots Wood

Distance
6½ miles (10.5km)

Height gain
785 feet (240m)

Approximate time
3 hours

Route terrain
Undulating field and woodland paths and tracks

Parking
Cockshoots Wood car park off Cobblershill Lane, the turning for which is off A413 about 1¾ miles (2.8km) south of Wendover

OS maps
Landranger 165 (Aylesbury & Leighton Buzzard), Explorer 181 (Chiltern Hills North)

GPS waypoints
- SP 871 042
- **A** SP 871 035
- **B** SP 870 019
- **C** SP 862 016
- **D** SP 847 024
- **E** SP 846 034
- **F** SP 860 035
- **G** SP 870 036

Great Hampden and Little Hampden

Apart from one fairly steep climb near the end, this is a gently undulating walk through a peaceful, rolling and well-wooded landscape in the heart of the Chilterns. The route passes two remote and interesting churches at Great Hampden and Little Hampden.

Cockshoots Wood is crisscrossed by a multiplicity of paths and tracks, but following the directions and bridleway waymark arrows as outlined here should keep you firmly on track.

Put your back to the lane at the car park entrance and look right to find and take the waymarked bridleway that disappears into the undergrowth. This well used and potentially muddy track snakes gently up through scrubby undergrowth to enter woodland. Bear right at the waymarked post and continue up the bridleway to follow the obvious grassy path between trees. Keep right at a junction with a track in the woods. In a further 100 yds or so is a complicated, waymarked junction of routes. Take the second left exit (bridleway) and follow the meandering path through the woods to emerge at a junction of lanes and paths **A**. The way is ahead along the lane, passing the corner-stile on your left. Keep right at the next lane, then at the sharp right bend keep ahead along the rougher track to reach another tarred lane, along which turn left.

At a public footpath sign turn left through a metal gate. Walk along a grassy, hedge-lined path and, emerging into a field, turn right to continue along the right-hand edge of the field, by a hedge on the right. The path later keeps along the right inside edge of woodland. On leaving the wood bear right along a track, then bear left, at a white arrow, going downhill along the right-hand edge of a field, by a hedge and trees on the right. Go through a hedge gap in the field corner and continue downhill across the middle of a field to a road.

Cross the road, take the lane ahead and at a public footpath sign turn right **B** up steps and walk along a narrow path between a wire fence on the left and a hedge on the right. Where the fence on the left ends, continue along the right-hand edge of a field. At the field corner the path continues ahead through woodland. Keep more or less in a straight line, later the path becomes more obvious. At a T-junction indicated by arrows on a tree trunk and a waymark, turn sharp left, head

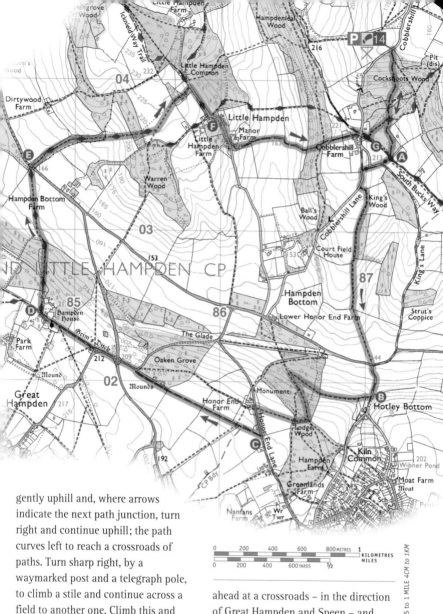

gently uphill and, where arrows indicate the next path junction, turn right and continue uphill; the path curves left to reach a crossroads of paths. Turn sharp right, by a waymarked post and a telegraph pole, to climb a stile and continue across a field to another one. Climb this and keep ahead on to a lane.

Turn left along the lane for 200 yds, and at a bridleway sign turn right **C** through a metal gate to walk along the right-hand edge of a field, by trees and then by a wire fence on the right. Keep in a straight line along the right-hand edge of a series of fields, going through another metal gate and finally continuing along the left-hand edge of woodland to a road. Bear left, keep

ahead at a crossroads – in the direction of Great Hampden and Speen – and

John Hampden

The most famous member of the Hampden family – lords of the manor – was John Hampden, a Parliamentary opponent of Charles I, whose refusal to pay ship money in 1641 helped to trigger the Civil War. He was killed in 1643 while fighting for the Parliamentary army. Hampden House was almost totally rebuilt in the 18th century.

SCALE 1:25000 or 2½ INCHES to 1 MILE 4CM to 1KM

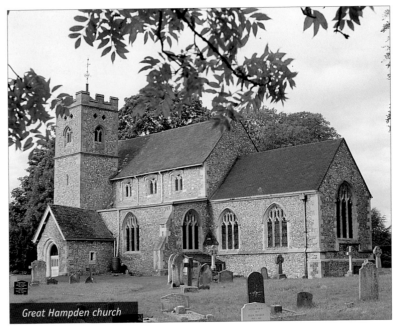

Great Hampden church

where the road bends sharply left, continue along a tarmac drive to pass between Hampden House on the right and Great Hampden church on the left.

Where the tarmac drive turns right into the grounds of the house, keep ahead through a gate and immediately turn right over a stile **D**. Walk across a field, passing the front of Hampden House, and head gently downhill through mixed woodland. Continue straight across a field to climb a stile on to a road **E**. Cross the road and take the path ahead through more woodland. At a crossroads of paths turn right into a field. Continue straight across the field heading towards a gate visible in the hedge at the far end of the second field.

Go through this gap, head uphill through a conifer wood, and on leaving the trees bear slightly left and walk across a field making for the trees on the far side. Here, at a waymark post, continue along a path, by a wire fence on the left – later the path becomes a drive – to a lane in the hamlet of Little

Hampden. Turn right, heading downhill along the lane to the tiny Little Hampden church, noted for its 15th-century timber-framed porch.

Opposite the church turn left **F**, at a public bridleway sign, along a track that heads downhill, meandering along the left-hand edge of a field, and then climbs up to the edge of woodland. Pass through a gap in the trees to head uphill through the wood, keeping on the main path all the while; at the top emerge from the trees and continue between wire fences to a metal gate. Go through the gate and keep ahead between wire fences, then on a concrete path beside a beech hedge, passing to the left of farm outbuildings. On reaching a lane turn left for several paces, then right, following the South Bucks Way and the Chiltern Way. When a tarmac drive sweeps right, turn left **G** at the Chiltern Way sign into woods and almost immediately fork left. Follow the path for about 300yds to a junction. Keep ahead here and retrace your steps to the car park. ●

Cookham, Winter Hill and Cock Marsh

This walk embraces woodland, marsh and meadow; extensive views over the Thames Valley; pleasant and easy riverside walking, and an attractive village. The first part of the route is along the banks of the Thames by Cock Marsh. This is very much Stanley Spencer country: the artist spent most of his life in Cookham, and the village and surrounding area were the inspiration for many of his paintings. The walk then climbs to Winter Hill, a fine viewpoint overlooking the valley and Buckinghamshire beyond, before entering Quarry Wood, thought to be the model for the Wild Wood in the children's classic The Wind in the Willows.

Start
Cookham Moor

Distance
6¾ miles (10.7km)

Height gain
395 feet (120m)

Approximate time
3 hours

Route terrain
Undulating field and woodland paths, lanes and Thames Path

Parking
National Trust car park at Cookham Moor, just west of Cookham. Alternative parking in Cookham village

OS maps
Landranger 175 (Reading & Windsor), Explorer 172 (Chiltern Hills East)

GPS waypoints
- SU 892 853
- Ⓐ SU 897 854
- Ⓑ SU 881 870
- Ⓒ SU 864 857
- Ⓓ SU 870 851
- Ⓔ SU 881 861
- Ⓕ SU 889 855

From the car park take the path parallel to the road and follow the High Street. There are several pubs along here – including **The Crown**, **The King's Arms** and the **Bel and the Dragon** – and a café, **Infusions**. At the T-junction turn left and briefly walk along the road to Church Gate and a sign for the 11th century church. Bear left here Ⓐ and follow the path through the churchyard, keeping the church on your right, to a wrought iron gate. Beyond it follow the path to the Thames riverbank.

Turn left (signposted Chiltern Way Berkshire loop) and head upstream, passing Cookham Reach Sailing Club. Go through a galvanised gate on to Cock Marsh and over to the right the gardens of houses at Bourne End reach down to the water's edge. Pass beneath the Bourne End railway bridge and alongside **The Bounty**, a popular riverside pub. Continue beside a line of houses, go through a gate and across open meadow and marsh, with the riverbank becoming more rural and less crowded.

At Ferry Cottage swing away from the Thames and follow a grassy path beside farmland. In front of a galvanised gate, turn left to follow a footpath Ⓑ, passing through a gate on the far side of the field. Keep ahead for a few paces and then bear right at the signpost, heading diagonally up the slope. Go through a galvanised kissing-gate, pass beneath a canopy of trees and bear right at the Chiltern Way/public footpath sign. At the T-junction turn left up Stonehouse Lane to the next junction. Turn right, passing a National Trust sign for Winter Hill.

Follow the grassy path parallel to the road and as the latter begins to curve left, make for a gap in the foliage a few yards

The view from Winter Hill

from it. Pass through the trees and then turn right at a drive. On reaching the entrance to Rivendell, go forward to join a narrow path running through the trees. Pass alongside the wall of the house and continue into the woods. Farther on, the path forks. Keep right and continue between trees and foliage.

At the road **C** cross over, ignore the path in front of you and turn right, down to the next path on the left which has a Woodland Trust sign. Climb some steps into Quarry Wood, part of Bisham Woods, which consists of 383 acres of woodland in the care of the Woodland Trust. The woods were once part of a vast estate owned by Bisham Abbey. Part of it was once included in the Royal Forest of Windsor in which Elizabeth I used to ride.

Continue on the waymarked path and at the second post swing left. Follow the path in line with tall, blue-topped wooden posts and soon you reach an information board. At the road turn right into Grubwood Lane and follow it with a row of houses on the left. Beyond them bear left at a wide drive (King's Coppice Farm) and follow a field edge path with the drive on your immediate

left. When the drive bends left, follow the path as it runs diagonally left up the field slope. On reaching the field corner, take the path on the right through trees and undergrowth to reach the garden of the **Jolly Farmer** pub.

From the front of the pub **D**, walk down the lane, keeping the church of St

John the Baptist on the right. Follow the road round to the right by the war memorial and pass the village green. Turn left into Popes Lane and follow it as it descends to a sign for Cookham Dean Bottom.

Turn sharp right here, bear right at the next junction (Dean Lane) and follow the road to Alleyns Lane. Turn left here, walk along to Hillgrove Farm and at the junction with Bradcutts Lane go straight across to join a footpath.

Follow the enclosed path, go through a kissing-gate and keep along the field edge, beside a hedge, to the next gate, leading on to a lane **E**. Go straight across, passing to the left of the entrance to September Grange, and follow the path along the field edge to a waymark. Bear right, following the Chiltern Way across a golf course. When the hedge ends go straight on across the fairways, pass to the left of a building and on over a bridge across the railway line. Turn immediately right, skirt the fairways and join an enclosed path, heading towards houses and rooftops. Join a track and as you reach the road turn sharp left by the entrance to Fiveways **F**. Follow an enclosed path, go through a gate and keep right, following a clear path back to the start.

SCALE 1:25000 or 2½ INCHES to 1 MILE 4CM to 1KM

| 0 | 200 | 400 | 600 | 800 METRES | 1 |
| 0 | 200 | 400 | 600 YARDS | ½ | KILOMETRES MILES |

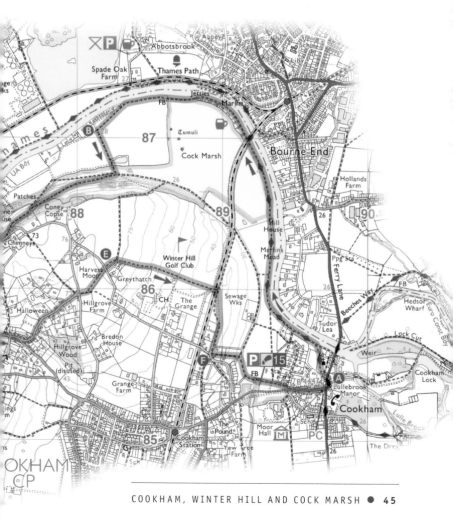

walk 16

Abingdon and Sutton Courtenay

Much of this route involves long stretches of pleasant walking by the riverside, following the Thames as it makes a large curve to the east and south of Abingdon. The terrain is flat throughout, the views are wide and extensive, and there is an opportunity to visit two villages as well as to explore Abingdon itself, a fine historic town.

Start
Abingdon Bridge

Distance
7½ miles (11.8km)

Height gain
80 feet (25m)

Approximate time
3 hours

Route terrain
Thames Path, lanes and field path

Parking
Rye Farm car park (Pay and display) on the south side of Abingdon Bridge

OS maps
Landranger 164 (Oxford), Explorer 170 (Abingdon, Wantage & Vale of White Horse)

GPS waypoints
- 🖊 SU 500 967
- Ⓐ SU 503 947
- Ⓑ SU 505 943
- Ⓒ SU 506 943
- Ⓓ SU 508 947
- Ⓔ SU 511 953
- Ⓕ SU 528 960
- Ⓖ SU 525 969

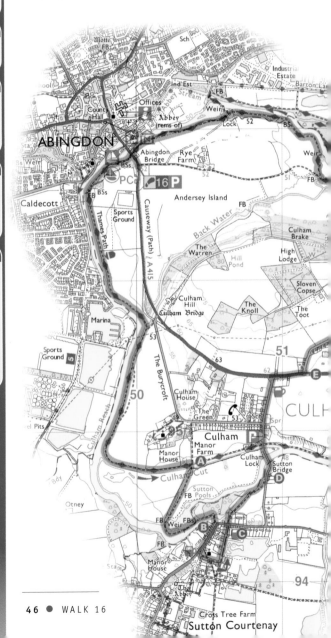

Abingdon

Abingdon has always been an important crossing point on the Thames. The bridge and causeway which link it to Culham were built by a local guild of merchants in the 15th century, to improve communications and overcome the problem of flooding, and thus ensure the town's continued prosperity. Of the great Benedictine abbey, once one of the wealthiest in the country, only fragments survive but Abingdon possesses some impressive churches and a particularly grand and dignified 17th century town hall, possibly influenced by Wren. There are also attractive views of the town from the opposite bank of the river.

follow Culham Cut, an arm of Thames. To the left the picture[ ] grouping of the manor house a[ ] church at Culham can be seen acro[ ] the meadows.

At a footbridge turn left to visit Culham; the route continues by turning right **Ⓐ** over the footbridge and taking the path ahead across fields. On meeting the main river again the path crosses a footbridge above a weir, continues through trees and then follows the curve of the river sharply to the left to cross three successive footbridges above weirs. Keep ahead along a shady riverside path which bends sharply right and passes through a metal kissing-gate into Sutton Courtenay **Ⓑ**. This attractive village has a large tree-lined green and a fine medieval church that retains some Norman work. Two famous men are buried here: Herbert Asquith and George Orwell.

Either bear left if wishing to omit the 'loop' through the village or turn right along Church Street passing the **George and Dragon** pub and the church. Turn left immediately beyond it along a narrow tarmac path, between a cottage on the right and the churchyard wall on the left. Pass through a metal barrier on to a track, and at a T-junction of tracks turn left along a wide concrete drive, still alongside the churchyard wall, and follow the drive to a road **Ⓒ** by **The Fish**, rejoining the shorter route which omitted the village. Cross the road, to a footpath sign (Thames Path ½ mile) and continue along the concrete drive

🖊 Begin by walking across the grass to the river, turn left along the riverside path and follow it for about 1¾ miles to Culham. This is a pleasant stretch of the Thames across unspoilt riverside meadows, and the path is tree-shaded in places. At times Didcot power station can be glimpsed ahead. Eventually the path bends to the left to

Sutton Courtenay

which bears right to a stile. Climb it, continue along the left-hand edge of a meadow, soon rejoining the riverbank and following it to Sutton Bridge. Just before the bridge look out for a public footpath sign on the right, where you pass through a gate on to a road **D**.

Turn left, cross first Sutton Bridge and then another one over Culham Cut and keep ahead along the road for ¼ mile to a T-junction. Turn right, in the Dorchester direction, along the main road – there is a path beside it – and take the first side road on the left **E**, Thame Lane, signposted to the European School. The road soon curves right and continues in a straight line for one mile, becoming a narrow lane after passing the school entrance and then a rough track after passing Warren Farm. All around there are wide views across the Oxford Plain, and to the right Wittenham Clumps can be seen in the foreground, with the line of the Chilterns on the horizon.

Just before reaching a railway bridge turn left **F**, at a public footpath sign to Abingdon, and keep along the right-hand edge of fields on an enclosed path beside a railway line in its cutting on the right. Farther on the path joins a track and continues by the railway line. Cross a stile and once again continue on an enclosed path. Eventually you reach the Thames riverbank where you turn left **G** to continue along the field edge. The River Thames is just beyond the line of trees and bushes on the right; keep beside the river along the right-hand edge of fields. The path skirts the edge of fields until you meet a side channel. Turn away from the Thames here alongside the thick scrub and trees lining this wide stream to find the point where the path cuts right through a gap in the undergrowth. Cross the two narrow footbridges (slippery, beware), built across the site of Swift's Lock, the first erected on the Thames. Continue beyond the second bridge on a wide path across rough pasture to a flat tractor bridge, once across keep ahead right along the fieldside path.

Later you rejoin the Thames and turn left to follow it back to Abingdon Bridge, on a well-surfaced path, passing Abingdon Lock and continuing across meadows with good views of the town ahead. Pass under the bridge and the car park is to the left. ●

Henley-on-Thames and Hambleden

walk 17

Start
Henley-on-Thames

Distance
7¼ miles (11.6km)

Height gain
310 feet (95m)

Approximate time
3½ hours

Route terrain
Steady ascents/
descents on field and
woodland paths,
Thames Path

P Parking
Pay and display car
parks in Henley-on-
Thames

OS maps
Landranger 175
(Reading & Windsor),
Explorer 171 (Chiltern
Hills West)

GPS waypoints
SU 763 826
Ⓐ SU 765 826
Ⓑ SU 773 840
Ⓒ SU 784 840
Ⓓ SU 783 842
Ⓔ SU 785 850
Ⓕ SU 785 853
Ⓖ SU 783 864
Ⓗ SU 775 855
Ⓙ SU 772 855

The walk begins by crossing the Thames and heading up through Remenham Wood and across fields to the hamlet of Aston before descending to re-cross the river at Mill End. It then continues through a beautiful Chiltern valley to the picturesque and unspoilt village of Hambleden. From here the route climbs up through Ridge Wood, descends to the river again and follows an attractive riverside path back to Henley.

Henley-on-Thames Since the 18th century Henley has been one of the most popular and fashionable of Thames-side towns. It stands on a beautiful stretch of the river, crossed by a dignified 18th-century bridge, and has a number of attractive Georgian and earlier buildings. The famous annual regatta was first held in 1839. The mainly 15th-century church, whose tower dominates most of the views from the river, is situated near the bridge at the bottom end of Hart Street where the walk begins.

Start by crossing Henley Bridge, by the **Angel on the Bridge**, an historic pub, turn left along Remenham Lane Ⓐ, by the **Little Angel** pub, and at a public footpath sign turn right through a kissing-gate. Walk along a track that keeps close to the right-hand edge of a field, and where the track bends to the left, keep ahead to pass through a hedge gap, via a stile. Bear left to follow a faint but discernible path diagonally across a field to a Chilterns Way sign on the edge of trees in the far corner.

Head uphill through the trees, climb a stile and bear slightly left to continue along the top inside edge of the sloping woodland. On leaving the trees bear right and head across grass, veering away from the fence on the left, to climb a stile. Continue along a narrow path through Remenham Wood, first ascending and then descending gently to emerge from the woodland on to a track. Cross it and take the path ahead across a field, from which there are fine views over the Thames Valley to the Chilterns, to reach a public footpath sign and a lane on the far side. Turn left along the lane and, at a public footpath sign, turn right Ⓑ over a stile beside a metal gate and walk along a broad track across fields, later keeping by the right-hand edge of a belt of trees. Where the track turns left, keep right through a kissing-gate and head downhill through several paddocks to a road Ⓒ.

Turn left into the hamlet of Aston, turn left again at a junction by the **Flower Pot Hotel**, and at a public footpath sign turn right along a broad track ⓓ. Pass beside a metal gate and continue along this pleasant track as it winds across fields down to the River Thames. Bear left to follow the river to Hambleden Lock, turn right to cross the lock and continue across a long metal footbridge above a weir to the attractive building of Hambleden Mill, which is now converted into apartments. Continue along a tarmac path between fences and then turn left between cottages to the road at Mill End.

Turn right, take the first turning on the left ⓔ, signposted to Hambleden, Skirmett and Fingest, and follow the road for ¼ mile. At a junction for a minor road on the right to Rotten Row ⓕ, go through a gate, at a public footpath sign. Continue along the left-hand edge of a field, by a hedge on the left and keeping parallel with the road, through the lovely, gentle, wooded Hamble valley. Soon the cottages and church of Hambleden village are seen ahead. Go through a kissing-gate in the tapering far corner of a field, cross a track and go through a gate to continue across meadows bordering Hamble Brook on the right. At the far end of the meadows go through a metal kissing-gate on to a lane ⓖ. The village is to the right over the bridge. With its attractive brick and flint, red-tiled cottages, church, inn - **the Stag and Huntsman** - and manor house, Hambleden is the quintessential English village and one of the most delightful in the Chilterns.

The route continues to the left along the lane to the road. Cross the road and at a public footpath sign take the tarmac, hedge-lined path ahead, climbing steadily and later continuing

St Mary the Virgin The mainly 14th-century church at Hambleden has undergone several alterations; the western tower was added in the 18th century and the whole building was restored during the Victorian era. In the churchyard is the grave of W.H. Smith, founder of the chain of booksellers, who lived at nearby Greenlands.

through the attractive Ridge Wood. At a fork keep ahead, as you climb there are some fine views through the trees on the left over the Hamble valley, and at the top a superb view ahead over the Thames Valley. The path now descends to a crossroads of paths. Go over; ahead is a gate on the edge of the woodland. Go through the gate, continue along the left-hand edge of a field, by a hedge and wire fence on the left, climb a stile and keep in the same direction across the next field to cross two more stiles to a gate and bridleway sign by a road ⓗ.

Turn right along the road – there is a footpath beside it – for ¼ mile. At a public footpath sign turn left ⓙ over a stile to follow a rather indistinct but straight path across parkland, crossing in turn a tarmac drive and three footbridges before reaching the riverbank. Follow the Thames back to Henley, crossing a series of footbridges and passing first Temple Island to the left, Remenham church on the opposite bank of the river, and Fawley Court, the latter built in the late 17th century by Wren and situated at the end of a poplar-lined channel that gives it a Dutch air. Towards the end of this section there are fine views ahead of Henley's bridge and church tower.

At the end of the last meadow turn right through a metal kissing-gate, walk along the left-hand edge of a field, by hedges and a wire fence on the left, and continue along an enclosed and partially tree-lined path to go through a metal gate on to a road. Turn left into Henley, bear left at a mini roundabout and continue along Bell St as far as the market place, just to the left of Henley Town Hall. Here turn left down Hart Street to return to the start. ●

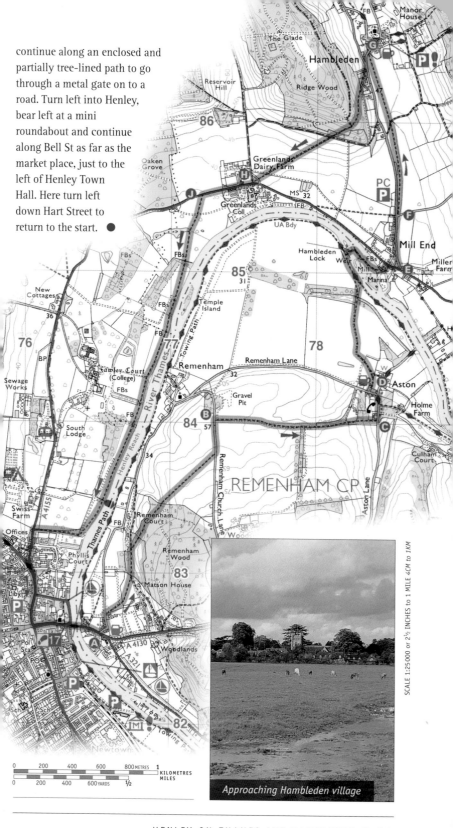

Approaching Hambleden village

SCALE 1:25000 or 2½ INCHES to 1 MILE 4CM to 1KM

walk 18

Runnymede and Windsor Great Park

Start

Bishopsgate entrance to Windsor Great Park

Distance

7¼ miles (11.6km)

Height gain

410 feet (125m)

Approximate time

3½ hours

Route terrain

Steady climb through Cooper's Hill woodland; lanes and generally broad parkland tracks and rides

P Parking

At the end of Bishopsgate Road. Follow signs to Savill Gardens from A328 at Engelfield Green and turn along Bishopsgate Road

OS maps

Landranger 176 (West London), Explorer 160 (Windsor, Weybridge & Bracknell)

GPS waypoints

SU 978 722
Ⓐ SU 984 723
Ⓑ SU 991 723
Ⓒ SU 997 728
Ⓓ TQ 002 726
Ⓔ SU 996 712
Ⓕ SU 988 713
Ⓖ SU 979 712
Ⓗ SU 977 707
Ⓙ SU 967 726

Historic interest is interwoven with riverside meadows, woodland and parkland on this varied walk. Runnymede is the site of one of the best-known events in English history, the signing of Magna Carta, and there is a memorial to the occasion there. Nearby is a memorial to President Kennedy, and the Commonwealth Air Forces Memorial is on Cooper's Hill above. Windsor Great Park was originally carved from Windsor Forest and its 3,000 acres (1,215 ha) are the main remnants of what was once a huge area of forest that stretched across much of Surrey and Berkshire. Towards the end of the walk is a memorable view from the Copper Horse, the equestrian statue of George III, looking down the Long Walk to the dramatic outline of Windsor Castle.

Start by walking away from the park entrance along Bishopsgate Road, passing the **Fox and Hounds**. Bear left along Crimp Hill, take the first turning on the right Ⓐ, Ridgemead Road, and where the road bends right, keep ahead across grass (cutting a corner) to turn left along the A328. At a public footpath sign turn right Ⓑ through a metal gate and walk along a tarmac, tree-lined track through grounds belonging to Brunel University. Keep ahead at a fork and on reaching a gate on the right and a National Trust sign for Runnymede, continue ahead on a rough track – heading downhill to reach the John F. Kennedy memorial. Continue past this, descending a series of steps through woods. Go through a gate on the edge of the trees and turn right Ⓒ on to a grassy path along the right-hand edge

The Magna Carta Memorial

The Copper Horse in Windsor Great Park

of Runnymede Meadows to the Magna Carta Memorial, a gift of the American Bar Association, accessible via a gate on the right. It commemorates the signing in these meadows of Magna Carta by a reluctant King John in 1215.

At the memorial turn left along a straight path across the meadow, by a wire fence on the right, and cross the A308 to the Thames opposite Magna Carta Island. Turn right along the river, and when you draw level with the Commonwealth Air Forces Memorial up in the trees to the right, bear right to a Memorial sign by the road **D**. Cross over to a kissing-gate, walk ahead to the far side of the meadow and continue on a narrow path between trees and bushes. Go through two kissing-gates and continue up a lengthy flight of steps – the going quite steep in places. At the top, by a National Trust sign for Cooper's Hill Woods, go through a kissing-gate and turn right along a tarmac drive and a short distance ahead the drive bears right to the Commonwealth Air Forces Memorial. This impressive and dignified monument to the airmen who died in World War II stands in immaculate grounds and commands fine views over the Thames Valley.

At the point where the drive bears right, go left through a metal kissing-gate, at a public footpath sign, and walk along a tarmac path by the left-hand edge of a sports field. The path later runs between walls and fences, turning first right and then left and continues as a rough, enclosed path to a road. Cross the road, go through the metal barrier opposite and continue along an enclosed tarmac path to pass through another metal barrier on to a road **E**.

Turn right, and at a junction just ahead bear left along Barley Mow Road to a crossroads. Cross over, continue along the left side of Engelfield Green, passing the **Barley Mow** pub. At a fork keep left along Northcroft Road, following the road around a left- and a right-hand bend. At the next left bend turn right at a footpath sign **F**. Follow the path between hedges and trees. Go through a kissing-gate and continue over a stream via a footbridge. Beyond is a field where the path forks. Keep left and go diagonally across the pasture to a kissing-gate. Join an enclosed path between wooden fencing and hedging. Pass a kissing-gate and public footpath sign on the right and descend to cross a track between kissing-gates. Follow the path ahead through trees to the next kissing-gate and continue ahead on the track, passing in front of a row of houses, to a road just to the right of the Sun pub **G**. Bear left along Wick Lane, passing in front of **The Sun**, and in just over ¼ mile reach the coach park entrance to Savill Gardens **H**, a colourful 35-acre garden begun in 1932, well worth a visit.

Take the turning, keep the entrance to the **Savill Building** on the right (coffee shop and restaurant here) and walk ahead towards the obelisk that commemorates the Duke of Cumberland, son of George II and victor of Culloden. In front of the obelisk turn right along a track which passes to the right of the Obelisk Pond and crosses a bridge over the end of it. Keep ahead along a broad grassy ride, between the boundary of Savill Gardens on the right and the open expanse of Smith's Lawn on the left, making for the brick lodge of Cumberland Gate in front. At a road junction in front of the lodge, turn right through a gate and then turn left to continue in the same direction as

before, keeping right at an immediate fork. Follow the grassy path and on reaching a tarmac drive turn left along it towards Cumberland Lodge, then bear right along a track, passing to the right of a tennis court and continuing to a road junction.

Turn left, and then turn right along a track that heads downhill through trees, by a fence on the right, passing to the right of Ox Pond to emerge into a more open landscape. Continue along the broad, hedge-lined, grass ride towards the Copper Horse statue straight ahead. Over to the right Royal Lodge can be seen. Go through a metal gate in a deer

fence and keep ahead to the huge, equestrian statue of George III erected in 1831 on Snow Hill. This is the highest point in the park and a magnificent viewpoint over the woods and lawns of the park, the Thames Valley and especially along the impressive three-mile avenue of the Long Walk, created by Charles II in 1680, to the profile of Windsor Castle on the skyline.

In front of the statue **J** turn right along a grassy track into woodland, bear left on meeting another track and continue straight ahead along a grassy ride to the right of a bridge and the road below. From here there are more fine views of Windsor Castle.

On meeting the road turn right alongside it, go through a metal gate in the deer fence again and bear left along a tree-lined path to rejoin the road in front of the Bishopsgate entrance. Go through the gate to return to the start. ●

SCALE 1:25000 or 2½ INCHES to 1 MILE 4CM to 1KM

Longworth and Hinton Waldrist

Start
Longworth

Distance
7¾ miles (12.4km)

Height gain
180 feet (55m)

Approximate time
3½ hours

Route terrain
Lanes, Thames Path and field paths

P Parking
Laneside (with consideration) in Longworth, in the vicinity of the parish noticeboard

OS maps
Landranger 164 (Oxford), Explorers 170 (Abingdon, Wantage & Vale of Whitehorse) and 180 (Oxford)

GPS waypoints

✎ SU 389 993
Ⓐ SU 390 999
Ⓑ SP 389 011
Ⓒ SP 366 008
Ⓓ SP 353 996
Ⓔ SU 375 991

One of the delights of walking by the River Thames is witnessing the river's constantly changing character and scenery. The upper reaches tend to be remote and undiscovered and the stretch of river explored on this walk is no exception. North of picturesque Longworth, the route coincides with the Thames Path, following the river upstream for several miles to the charmingly named Chimney Meadows and Tenfoot Bridge. Here the walk bids farewell to the river to head for Hinton Waldrist, another delightful Oxfordshire village.

✎ Turn into Tucks Lane, pass a sign 'no through road to River Thames' and the **Blue Boar** pub and continue through the village. Along this stretch are various attractive stone-built properties, including Sunnymeade House and New Barn. Pass Princes Farm and note a striking house called Coltons on the right. Follow the tarmac lane as it bends right and begins to descend between trees, hedgerows and fields.

On reaching a junction by a telegraph pole, with a Thames Path sign attached to it, and a bridleway to Newbridge on the right, turn left Ⓐ. After a few paces turn right in front of the entrance to Tucks Mead and follow the track north between trees and foliage. Begin a gradual ascent towards the woodland of Harrowdown Hill, keep to the right of it and then begin a gentle descent. Continue on an enclosed path between high hedges and then straight on along the left edge of a field to a narrow gap in the corner. Pass between trees to reach a kissing-gate. Go straight on in the meadow, arriving at the Thames near a kissing-gate and Thames Path post on the riverbank Ⓑ.

Follow the river upstream, with the Thames close by on the right, before spotting the buildings of

Shifford, a remote little community on the opposite bank of the river. Follow the signs for the Thames Path at Shifford Lock, crossing over to the south bank of Shifford Lock Cut. Cross again at the next bridge **C** and follow the Thames once more, this time along the north bank of the river. Keep to the towpath for some way, the Thames meandering through a pastoral, quintessentially English landscape with few signs of habitation.

On reaching Tenfoot Bridge **D**, recross the river to the south bank and follow the path south to the n͟ junction. Turn left here and h͟ the path between fields and m͟ At the next junction turn right fo͟ 100yds, then pass through a gap in the field boundary to follow a grassy track alongside the perimeter. Follow it as it bends left and runs across farmland to some trees. Continue on the track in the next field, keeping the trees on the right. Pass alongside the buildings of

The Blue Boar at Longworth

Duxford Farm and follow the lane. Pass a bridleway on the left to Chimney and continue in the direction of Hinton Waldrist. The road climbs between trees before passing a cemetery on the left.

Airey Neave

Near the cemetery's main gate is the grave of Airey Neave (1916-79), a famous World War II hero who escaped from Colditz and later became a prominent Conservative politician. Neave opposed the withdrawal of British forces from Northern Ireland and was assassinated by the INLA two months before Margaret Thatcher came to power.

Continue on the road as it swings right by stone walls, now approaching Hinton Waldrist. Pass the entrance to Hinton Manor, then the church of St Margaret of Antioch. Turn left opposite the entrance **E** and follow the lane, passing The Grange. When the lane bends right, continue ahead along a bridleway and look for glimpses of Longworth church ahead. Pass a paddock and in the distance is Harrowdown Hill, featured early in the walk. Veer right, then left to join a drive running alongside several barns and stables. Longworth Manor edges into view now. Follow the drive between beech trees, then down into Longworth. At the junction turn left by Rose Cottage and return to the centre of the village. ●

Longworth

John Fell, Dean of Christ Church and Bishop of Oxford, was born in Longworth in the early 17th century. One of his students based a famous Latin epigram on him following a reprimand:

I do not love thee Doctor Fell
The reason why I cannot tell
But this I know and know full well
I do not love thee Doctor Fell

The novelist R.D.Blackmore, best known for Lorna Doone, was born in the village in 1825. The delightful thatched Blue Boar pub in Longworth was once a bakery and an Elizabethan alehouse.

The clock tower at Chesham

walk 20

Aldbury, Ivinghoe Beacon and Ashridge

This outstanding walk starts in a picturesque village, proceeds along the Chiltern escarpment to Ivinghoe Beacon – one of the highest viewpoints in the Chilterns – and returns through part of the magnificent woodlands of the National Trust's Ashridge Estate. There are several climbs but the paths are good, the route easy to follow, and the views superb all the way.

Start
Aldbury

Distance
7½ miles (11.8km)

Height gain
805 feet (245m)

Approximate time
4 hours

Route terrain
Good field and woodland paths and tracks

Parking
Laneside (with consideration) in Aldbury. Alternatively, car parks at Pitstone Hill **B** and Bridgewater Monument **F**

OS maps
Landranger 165 (Aylesbury & Leighton Buzzard), Explorer 181 (Chiltern Hills North)

GPS waypoints
- SP 964 124
- **A** SP 962 124
- **B** SP 955 149
- **C** SP 960 163
- **D** SP 959 168
- **E** SP 963 155
- **F** SP 970 131

> **Aldbury** All the ingredients that make up the classic English village scene are present in Aldbury: charming brick and half-timbered cottages (some thatched) and a pub - the Greyhound - grouped around a triangular green; duck pond, stocks and whipping-post standing on the green; and a short distance away a medieval church. The village is set against the backdrop of the beech woods of Ashridge. Aldbury has frequently been used as a film set.

Start by walking along the road in the Tring direction, passing the church, and at a public footpath sign to Pitstone Hill turn right through a gate **A**. Head across to go through a second gate, continue along the left-hand edge of a field, by farm buildings on the left, but before reaching the end of the buildings look out for a gate on the left. Immediately turn right along a narrow enclosed path, go through two galvanised gates and continue along a path between wire fences and hedges.

At a path junction go over to a kissing-gate and continue across part of a golf course, following a fairly obvious grassy path and keeping in the same direction as before – a series of yellow-waymarked posts aid route-finding. Later, keep along the left edge of trees and a hedge to go through a kissing-gate in the top right-hand corner of a field, and continue between trees, bushes and scrub to a finger-post at a path junction. Bear left and then turn right up a flight of steps, here joining the Ridgeway.

Follow the acorn symbol Ridgeway waymarks over Pitstone Hill. Initially the route passes through woodland, but after passing through a kissing-gate, it continues over open downland with some fine views to the left over the Vale of Aylesbury, even though the dominant feature is Pitstone Cement Works. The path later descends and curves gradually to the right, keeping close to a wire fence on the right, finally bearing left to a stile in front of Pitstone Hill car park. On this

Looking towards Ivinghoe Beacon

uphill between trees to join a track. Bear left along the track, which curves left to reach an open grassy area beside the road. Turn right alongside hedges on the right, parallel to the road, and at the end of this grassy area turn right **E** along a track signposted 'Ashridge Estate. Restricted access, Clipper Down Cottage only' and waymarked with a National Trust green horseshoe bridlepath waymark, which is the waymark to follow for the next mile or so.

Almost the whole of the remainder of the walk is through part of the splendid beech woods of the Ashridge Estate, over 4,000 acres (1,620 ha) of open grassland, commons and woodlands belonging to the National Trust. Follow the track through this attractive woodland, taking care to keep on the main track all the while, to Clipper Down Cottage. Go through a gate, pass to the right of the cottage and continue along another track: at intervals there are superb views to the right from these wooded slopes across the flatter country of the vale. Pass to the left of a log cabin and soon after crossing a footbridge you reach the Bridgewater Monument **F**, erected in 1832 in memory of the third Duke of Bridgewater, the great canal builder and owner of Ashridge. The view from the top is well worth the climb.

Keep ahead past the monument to join a track in front of the National Trust shop, visitor centre and **Brownlow Café**. Turn right and follow the track downhill through woodland. At a fork take the right-hand lower track to continue downhill to a road and turn right for a short distance to return to the centre of Aldbury village.

descent the escarpment and next part of the route can be seen stretching ahead to Ivinghoe Beacon.

Go through a gate, pass through the car park **B**, cross a lane and take the path opposite that heads straight across a large field. Continue across the next field. The path ascends before curving left to a stile. Do not climb it but pass to the left of it and head across, keeping parallel to a hedge and wire fence on the right, to a Ridgeway marker post on the edge of woodland. Continue through the trees and on emerging from them keep ahead downhill, by a wire fence on the right. Turn right through a gate in the fence, head uphill through an area of scrub and bushes, and then continue downhill. Bear left down to the corner of a road **C**. Cross the road and follow the left-hand one of the two tracks ahead up to the summit of Ivinghoe Beacon, marked by a triangulation pillar **D**. This outlying spur of the Chiltern range, 764ft (233m) high, gives a magnificent panorama over the Vale of Aylesbury, along the Chiltern escarpment from Dunstable Downs to Coombe Hill and across to the slopes of Ashridge Park.

Retrace your steps to the road **C**, cross over and then turn left, at a National Trust marker post, along a pleasant path that initially keeps parallel to the road on the left, heading

Ibstone, Turville and Fingest

There is a tranquillity and sense of remoteness about this walk which could place it in the more inaccessible parts of the Pennines or the depths of Dartmoor, but the landscape of beech woods and sweeping dry chalk valleys is unmistakably that of the Chilterns. The feeling of remoteness is further reinforced by the two villages that are passed through en route: both Turville and Fingest are small, largely unchanged and apparently timeless villages with distinctive and interesting churches, tucked away in a quiet valley.

Start
Ibstone Common

Distance
7¾ miles (12.3km)

Height gain
855 feet (260m)

Approximate time
4 hours

Route terrain
Rolling downland and woodland tracks

P | Parking
Roadside parking beside Ibstone Common near Fox Country Inn, Restaurant and Hotel

OS maps
Landranger 175 (Reading & Windsor), Explorer 171 (Chiltern Hills West)

GPS waypoints
- SU 751 938
- Ⓐ SU 749 937
- Ⓑ SU 749 918
- Ⓒ SU 754 908
- Ⓓ SU 767 911
- Ⓔ SU 777 911
- Ⓕ SU 774 918
- Ⓖ SU 761 943

The walk starts just to the south of the **Fox Country Inn**, Restaurant & Hotel, where you take a grassy path along the edge of Ibstone Common, by trees on the right, ignoring the right of way sign here that directs you into the trees. Keep right at the fork. On the far side turn left Ⓐ to continue along the edge of the rough open common, cross a drive, keep ahead through trees and continue along a stony, hedge-lined track, passing to the left of a cottage and heading downhill to a tarmac drive.

Turn right along the drive, and on entering trees bear left at a public bridleway sign to follow the path which soon crosses the drive and then continues downhill through a narrow belt of woodland. At the bottom keep right at a fork for a few paces to a kissing-gate and go down the field slope to another gate. Pass through trees to a lane and turn left. Avoid a turning for Ashfield Farm and continue to the next road Ⓑ. Climb the stile opposite and head uphill across a field, by a wire fence on the right. All around are fine views over this lovely Chiltern valley. Climb a stile in the top corner of the field, bear slightly right to continue more steeply uphill up steps through woodland and at

Turville, deep in a fold of the Chilterns

the top turn left to follow a path through Idlecombe Wood.

The path, rough and sometimes overgrown at first, later broadens out and continues through beautiful beech woodland to a T-junction, where you turn right along a track which heads gently uphill to reach the top edge of woodland just in front of a brick wall and tarmac drive. Here turn left **C** through a gate and follow a straight grassy path across a field, passing to the left of Turville Court. Go through a gate, continue – with a lovely view over the valley ahead – and at the end of the field you start to descend, initially along the right-hand edge of woodland. Where the edge of the field curves left, keep straight ahead downhill across the field descending into the valley. At the bottom bear left along an enclosed path and continue down a road to a T-junction **D** in the centre of Turville village, an idyllic scene of old brick and half-timbered cottages grouped around a green, **The Bull and Butcher** pub and a restored late medieval church.

At the T-junction take the path opposite between cottages; a disused windmill, now a private residence, is on the top of the hill directly in front. Do not climb the stile immediately ahead but turn right through a gate and follow the grassy path across farmland. Head uphill across the corner of a field to a stile. Climb it, walk along a narrow path through a belt of trees to a gate and continue along the path. After crossing a lane continue through a gate and at a path junction bear right and, with a lovely view of the tower of Fingest church, head downhill to a gate leading on to a road on the edge of the village. Like Turville, Fingest has a picturesque collection of brick-and-timber houses, pub and church, but is even smaller. The church is one of the most unusual and interesting village churches in the Chilterns, noted for its plain, massive, twin-gabled Norman tower that looks out of proportion to the rest of the building.

Turn left into the village, passing to the right of the church. In front of the

Chequers Inn turn left along Chequers Lane **E**. After ½ mile, at a right-hand curve, go through a fence gap **F**, at public bridleway and footpath signs, and take the clear, wide path straight ahead. At a fork in front of a gate and stile, take the right-hand narrower path through a narrow belt of trees. Emerge from woodland and follow the clear enclosed path between hedging and fencing, cutting between fields. Continue along the right edge of a belt of woodland, keeping straight ahead on joining a track. Cross an intersection and pass a bridleway on the left. Cross a stile and disregard a second left-hand bridleway. Keep on the footpath, cross a track by some barns on the right and continue on the woodland path. Merge with another track at the point where a path crosses and continue along the bottom edge of Penley Wood.

Look out for white arrows on a tree trunk, and a little further on there is a fork **G**. Take the left-hand grassy path, soon emerging from the trees to continue along the left-hand edge of a field. At the end of the field cross a track, keep ahead steadily uphill through more trees, and on leaving this final area of woodland you join a farm track. Ahead are the houses of Ibstone. Follow the track to a road and turn right to return to the start. ●

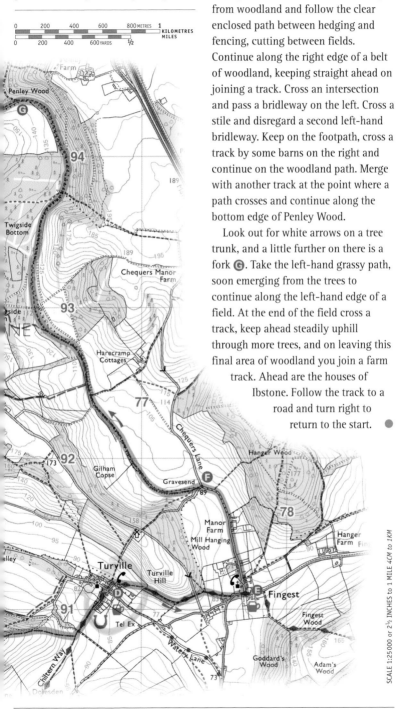

SCALE 1:25000 or 2½ INCHES to 1 MILE 4CM to 1KM

walk 22

Start
Wendover

Distance
8 miles (12.7km)

Height gain
1,065 feet (325m)

Approximate time
4 hours

Route terrain
Woodland and undulating downland paths

P Parking
High Street car park in Wendover. Alternatively, Wendover Station is passed soon after the start of the walk

OS maps
Landranger 165 (Aylesbury & Leighton Buzzard), Explorer 181 (Chiltern Hills North)

GPS waypoints
SP 869 078
Ⓐ SP 863 074
Ⓑ SP 849 067
Ⓒ SP 843 062
Ⓓ SP 836 066
Ⓔ SP 846 049
Ⓕ SP 854 050
Ⓖ SP 857 060

Coombe Hill and Chequers

This is one of the great walks of the Chilterns. From Wendover there is a long and steady climb to the summit of Coombe Hill, the highest and one of the most magnificent viewpoints in the Chilterns (the highest point is actually in Wendover Woods a short distance away). The route then drops down the steep face of the escarpment and continues across fields to the village of Ellesborough, whose church tower is visible from Coombe Hill. The rest of the walk follows an undulating route, punctuated by delightful woodland, and passes Chequers, the Prime Minister's country residence, before the final descent into Wendover. There are a number of climbs but they are all gradual; in fact the steepest part of the walk is the descent from Coombe Hill.

The village of Wendover lies in an attractive position below the Chiltern escarpment and possesses some fine old cottages and Georgian houses; the church lies over ¼ mile to the south of the village centre.

Start at the bottom of the main street by the 19th-century clock tower, walk up the street, passing **The Red Lion**, and at the mini roundabout keep ahead, in the Ellesborough and Princes Risborough direction. Cross a railway and a road bridge, continue uphill along the road for ¼ mile and at a right-hand bend bear left, at public bridleway and Ridgeway signs, on to a path Ⓐ.

After a few paces, at a Bacombe Hill notice, the path forks; continue along the right-hand path, signposted Ridgeway, and at the next fork continue along the left-hand path to head up a series of steps. The well-defined path continues steadily uphill, sometimes between trees and bushes and at other times across open grassy areas, passing through three gates and on to the Boer War monument on the summit of Coombe Hill Ⓑ. From here, at 852ft (260m) the highest viewpoint in the Chilterns, a magnificent panorama unfolds over the Vale of Aylesbury, with Ellesborough church below. In clear weather the line of the Cotswolds is visible ahead, and to the right the Chiltern escarpment can be seen stretching away to Ivinghoe Beacon. This area was presented to the National Trust in 1918.

After passing the monument turn left, at a Ridgeway waymarked post with an acorn symbol, keeping just below the top of the escarpment and enjoying superb views to the right. About 100 yds before reaching woodland in front and at the point where the Ridgeway starts to bear left keep right at the fork along a faint, grassy path to a kissing-gate in the trees. Do not go through it but turn right and head steeply downhill to the bottom of the escarpment, by a wire fence on the left, to a crossroads of paths. The flat-topped hill ahead is Beacon Hill,

climbed later on the walk. At the crossroads keep ahead to go through a gate and continue along an enclosed track to a road by Coombe Hill Farm. Turn right, and at a public footpath sign turn left **C** to follow a clear path across a large field, later continuing along its right-hand edge, by a hedge on the right. Pass through a fence in the field corner and turn right along a hedge-lined track to a road opposite Ellesborough's imposing medieval church.

Turn left along a path above the road and then turn left **D** through a kissing-

SCALE 1:27777 or 2¼ INCHES to 1 MILE 3.6CM to 1KM

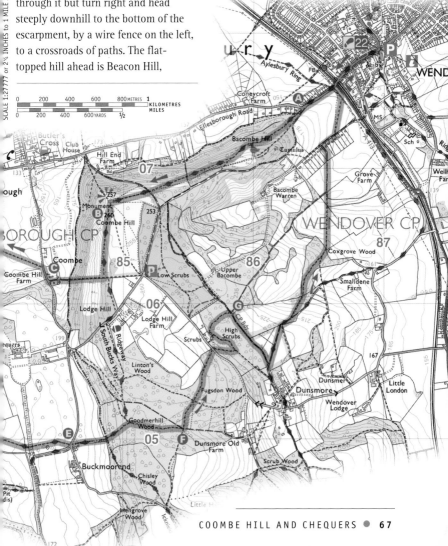

gate, at a public footpath sign, and take a path that heads diagonally and gently uphill across a field to a kissing-gate. Continue in the same direction along a rather indistinct path over the shoulder of Beacon Hill, later picking up a clear path which bears slightly left and continues above woodland on the right to a gate on the edge of Ellesborough Warren. Continue through the wood, go up a flight of steps, and at the top you emerge from the trees and continue across a field to the next belt of woodland. The path enters Whorley Wood and crosses a tarmac track to a gate. Keep ahead along the left-hand edge of a field, beside trees and a fence. Follow the boundary as it curves left and look for a gate near the field corner.

Go through it to rejoin the Ridgeway and continue along the left-hand edge of Maple Wood. Over to the left is Chequers, a large 16th-century house given to the nation in 1921 by Viscount and Viscountess Lee of Fareham, to be used as a country retreat for prime ministers. The views from here across the valley to the wooded slopes on the other side are very pleasant. At a Ridgeway sign turn left through a gate, walk across a field, go through three more gates, with Victory Drive, a beech lined avenue planted under the instructions of Winston Churchill, in between and follow the path to a gate leading out to the road **E**. Cross the road and bear slightly left along the track opposite, at public bridleway and Ridgeway signs. At a fork follow the direction of a blue waymark and acorn symbol on a tree to take the right-hand track, which heads uphill to a junction of tracks and paths on the edge of Goodmerhill Wood.

Continue uphill through this beautiful woodland and, at the top, where the Ridgeway turns left, keep ahead to reach another crossroads of paths **F**. Turn left along a gently ascending path. Keep ahead through Fugsdon Wood, and continue downhill to a gate opening on to a lane.

Cross the lane, climb the stile opposite and continue through woodland to a T-junction of paths where you turn left. Keeping a sharp look-out for yellow arrows, follow a path that later bends right and continues through an area of immature birch trees to a stile into a fenced, cindered track **G**. Turn right along this and remain with it for about 550 yds to reach a junction of tracks. Here double back left along a wide track between wire and wood-rail fencing, which after a while enters Coxgrove Wood and bears right, heading gently downhill. Where an arrow on a tree indicates a fork, take the left-hand path to continue downhill through the wood, by a metal fence on the left.

Just after the fence ends, bear left – following the direction of a white arrow – to head uphill through the last of the many areas of beautiful woodland on this walk. On reaching an intersection in the trees, keep left and follow the path down to a stile. There is a fine open view ahead, looking towards Wendover. Climb the stile, bear slightly left to head downhill across a field, and continue uphill along a grassy path, to a gate. Walk along a fence-lined path and, where the fences end, continue between gardens and hedges, bearing left to a lane.

Turn right, and at a public footpath sign turn left over a stile and bear slightly right to walk across a field, heading down to a stile in the field corner, under pylon cables. Climb this, continue down an enclosed path to a road and turn right to return to Wendover village centre.

Whitchurch and Mapledurham

The River Thames at Pangbourne represents a timeless picture of pastoral English beauty. The elegant toll bridge spans the river just as it did one hundred years ago and along the banks are glimpses of pasture and wooded slopes rising to meet the horizon. This glorious scene forms the starting point for this spectacular walk which crosses the river into Oxfordshire and then heads east to the village of Mapledurham, famous for an imposing Elizabethan house which includes a priest hole and a private chapel. Nearby is a working 15th century corn mill. From here the walk climbs up through the valley, passing a welcome pub at Whitchurch Hill.

walk 23

Start
Pangbourne

Distance
8¼ miles (13.2km)

Height gain
575 feet (175m)

Approximate time
4 hours

Route terrain
Lanes and downland tracks

P Parking
Pangbourne Meadows long stay car park, by the Dolphin Centre

OS maps
Landranger 175 (Reading & Windsor), Explorer 159 (Reading)

GPS waypoints
- SU 636 767
- Ⓐ SU 651 778
- Ⓑ SU 672 772
- Ⓒ SU 663 782
- Ⓓ SU 652 784
- Ⓔ SU 640 788

Pangbourne Meadows

 Turn right out of the car park, cross the striking toll bridge over the Thames and head into Whitchurch. Pass **The Ferry Boat** and then turn right by **The Greyhound** pub into Eastfield Lane.

Pass a long line of houses and at the far end, when the road forks, by a sign for Lane End and Oakfield, keep left. After a few paces turn left at some wooden posts by Whitchurch Primary School. Pass some allotments and then swing right at a grassy expanse which is the setting for Whitchurch Thyme Maze, completed in 2006. Follow the path to the corner of the green and make for a gap in the hedge. On reaching the road turn right and soon you join a parallel path. Pass Bozedown Farm and when the road bends left for Goring, keep ahead at the wrought iron gates for Mapledurham and a sign for the Hardwick Estate **A**.

Over to the right the Thames can be seen winding through the countryside. Ahead the outline of Hardwick House is glimpsed. Elizabeth I stayed at this Tudor mansion and Charles I played bowls on the lawn. Pass Hardwick Stud and continue along the lane. When you

SCALE 1:25 000 or 2½ INCHES to 1 MILE *4CM to 1KM*

The Thames at Pangbourne

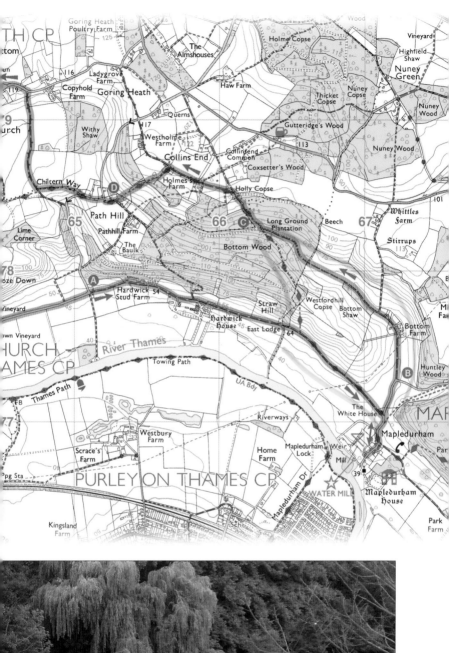

reach a junction of three tracks, with a private drive sign and neat hedging seen here, keep over to the left. On the left along this stretch are the remains of an old air-raid shelter for Hardwick House. Pass a pair of brick and timber cottages, then go through another wrought iron gate. Keep to the path and eventually you reach the road.

To visit Mapledurham village and tour the house, turn right. To continue the walk turn left here and when the road bends right, go straight on to follow the bridleway towards Bottom Farm and Goring Heath **B**.

Pass farm outbuildings and cottages and a path on the right and continue alongside woodland with fields on the right. Follow the track beside fencing towards more trees, pass between them and on reaching a junction, turn right by some laurel bushes to follow a bridleway **C**.

After a few paces, the track splits. Keep left and head up to Holly Copse Cottage. Continue as the track curves to the right towards a cottage and at this point veer left to a stile and gate. Go through the latter (Chiltern Way) and follow the path with fencing on the left. Go through a gate in the corner of the field and keep ahead at the Chiltern Way extension sign. Follow a tarmac lane between hedges and trees and turn left between some cottages, still following the signs for the Chiltern Way extension. Pass through a gate and go down the right edge of a paddock to a kissing-gate in the corner. Keep left in the next field and head down the side of it to the next gate, then downhill between trees and alongside fencing. Climb a steep slope to another gate, pass through trees to the road and turn right **D**.

Go left at the next junction and walk down the lane, passing a row of houses.

Bear right at the sign for Whitchurch Hill and follow the enclosed path to a kissing-gate. Continue ahead with hedge on the right and make for a gate in the field corner. Turn right to follow a broad path to the road and keep left. Pass a bus shelter and keep right at the sign for Hill Bottom. **The Sun**, on the right along here, offers the chance to take a break.

Resuming the walk, continue along the road, then turn left down Bridle Road and at the next junction **E**, turn right. Follow Goring Heath Road and at the junction, cross over to a parallel path and turn left. Follow the path beside the road all the way down to the war memorial, then cross over to continue on a parallel path to the left of the road. Walk down into Whitchurch, cross the toll bridge and return to the car park. ●

Mapledurham

Mapledurham and its timeless riverside setting present an idyllic picture. The village is one of only a few settlements in this area that have not fallen victim to urban expansion. The lack of a road bridge linking Mapledurham with Reading means that the village remains an isolated community tucked away down winding, leafy lanes on the edge of the Chilterns. Not surprisingly, its striking architecture and delightful setting have caught the eye of film and television producers over the years. The most memorable occasion dates back to the very hot summer of 1976 when Mapledurham became Studley Constable, a sleepy Norfolk village, for the wartime adventure thriller *The Eagle has Landed*, starring Michael Caine and Donald Sutherland. Some scenes were shot by the corn mill, others in the vicinity of Mapledurham House, which was completed by Sir Richard Blount for his Catholic family in the late 16th century.

West Wycombe, Hughenden and Bradenham

walk 24

Start
West Wycombe

Distance
8¼ miles (13.2km)

Height gain
1,015 feet (310m)

Approximate time
4 hours

Route terrain
Rolling downland and woodland paths and tracks

Parking
West Wycombe car park, adjacent to garden centre

OS maps
Landranger 165 (Aylesbury & Leighton Buzzard) and 175 (Reading and Windsor), Explorer 172 (Chiltern Hills East)

GPS waypoints
SU 826 947
Ⓐ SU 830 948
Ⓑ SU 842 960
Ⓒ SU 847 956
Ⓓ SU 849 953
Ⓔ SU 862 955
Ⓕ SU 853 966
Ⓖ SU 846 969
Ⓗ SU 825 970
Ⓙ SU 827 951

Three National Trust properties are linked by this walk. Two of them, Hughenden Manor and Bradenham Manor, have connections with Benjamin Disraeli; the third, West Wycombe House, is associated with Sir Francis Dashwood and the notorious 'Hell-Fire Club'. Between the three are some splendid areas of beech woodland and fine open views, the latter especially on the final stage of the walk along a wooded ridge path. Waymarking is generally good, but be particularly careful following the route directions across the thickly-wooded and potentially confusing Naphill Common. This is quite an energetic walk with plenty of ups and downs, but nothing particularly steep or strenuous.

Sir Francis Dashwood The main street of West Wycombe is lined with attractive 17th and 18th century brick and timber-framed houses. To the south of the village lies the house and park of the Dashwoods, to the north the church and Dashwood Mausoleum – all the work of the versatile and colourful Sir Francis Dashwood in the mid 18th-century. He was something of an enigma; on the one hand a cultured man of the arts responsible for the rebuilding of West Wycombe House and the redesigning of the park; on the other hand, founder of the Hell-Fire Club, a group of high-spirited young aristocrats who are alleged to have indulged in drunkenness, orgies and devil worship, in the caves at West Wycombe, at the golden ball on top of the church, or at nearby Medmenham Abbey.

Turn right out of the car park downhill towards the village and just before reaching the main road turn left along Church Lane. Walk uphill, passing the entrance to the Hell-Fire Caves and **café**, and just after a left-hand bend turn right Ⓐ, at a public footpath sign, and head downhill along the right-hand edge of a field, by a wire fence and line of trees on the right. Look out for a galvanised kissing-gate on the right, turn left and continue along the left-hand edge of a field to a kissing-gate leading on to a road.

Cross the road, climb a stile opposite and bear left diagonally across a field towards trees. Go through a gate, pass under a railway bridge, climb a stile and continue uphill along the left-hand edge of a field, by a wire fence on the left. Climb another stile and continue first through a narrow belt of trees and then along the left-hand edge of the next field. On the hill behind you there is a superb view of West Wycombe church and the Dashwood Mausoleum. Head downhill, cross a track, and continue uphill along a broad path towards a barn. Go through a fence gap, pass to the right of the barn and bear left along the lane ahead.

The lane leads gently downhill; at the bottom bear right, at a public footpath sign, on to a grassy path through an area of trees. On reaching an intersection, with a waymark post, a path running sharp left and a path bearing right uphill, take the latter route **B**. Continue through woodland, and on emerging from the trees keep along the left-hand edge of a field, by a hedge on the left.

Go through a metal kissing-gate in the field corner, keep ahead to pass between cottages, go through another metal kissing-gate and turn right to the road on the edge of Downley Common **C**.

Bear right, walk diagonally across the corner of the common – this part is a cricket field – and head downhill along the clear, grassy path ahead. Pass to the left of the Fleetwood Press, then bear right on to a wider track and continue downhill. Just after passing to the left of the Methodist church you reach a footpath sign **D**; here turn sharp left (not half-left) on to a path that soon heads into trees. At a path junction bear right, in the direction of the blue

waymark towards Hughenden Valley, and continue along the valley bottom through glorious woodland. On emerging from the trees keep ahead across sloping fields along a path between fencing and hedging to re-enter more woodland. The path winds gently uphill and, after leaving the trees once more, it continues along a tarmac drive, between walls, passing the entrance to Hughenden Manor (NT **restaurant**).

Continue downhill and a lovely view opens up on the right of the Hughenden valley, with the church below. Just after passing a cattle-grid turn left **E** through a gate, at a public footpath sign for Naphill, on to a path that winds uphill through trees. Keep ahead at a

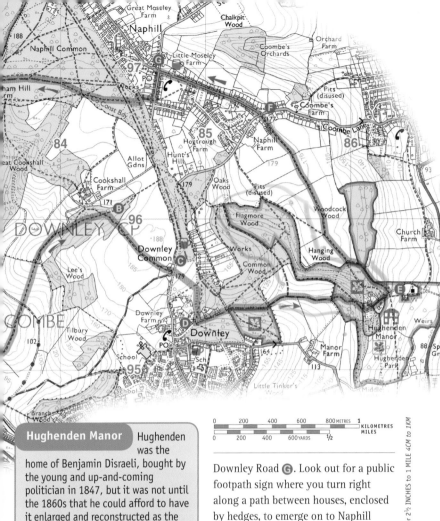

SCALE 1:25 000 or 2½ INCHES to 1 MILE 4CM to 1KM

Hughenden Manor Hughenden was the home of Benjamin Disraeli, bought by the young and up-and-coming politician in 1847, but it was not until the 1860s that he could afford to have it enlarged and reconstructed as the present imposing mansion. Inside it is full of pictures and mementoes of the great statesman, and remains much as he left it when he died in 1881. Nearby is the small church, mainly a Victorian rebuilding, in which Disraeli is buried.

path junction, and continue along the left-hand edge of a field, between trees and wire fencing. At the path junction turn right. Continue along a hedge-lined track which eventually leads on to a road on the edge of Naphill **F**.

Bear left along the road through the mainly modern village, passing **The Wheel** pub on the right and the **Bon Ami Café** on the left, and turn left along

Downley Road **G**. Look out for a public footpath sign where you turn right along a path between houses, enclosed by hedges, to emerge on to Naphill Common. Keep straight ahead for about 60yds to a path junction and go straight on to a path intersection by a waymark post. Turn left. Keep ahead along the bridleway through the beautiful, thickly wooded common, ignoring all side paths, to reach another path junction by a field corner on the left. Bear right to head slightly downhill into a shallow hollow and then continue gently up to a T-junction of paths by a waymarked post.

Bear left along a track to continue through woodland, following blue waymarks and keeping more or less in a straight line, eventually joining a broad, stony track. Head downhill, take the

Hughenden Manor, home of Disraeli

right-hand track at a fork, continue down to a waymarked post and bear left between the edge of woodland on the left and a brick wall bordering the grounds of Bradenham Manor on the right. The track winds down-hill to emerge on to the green at Bradenham. Most of this delightful village, with flint cottages and restored medieval church overlooking the large green, is owned by the National Trust. The 17th-century manor house, now a conference centre, was once the home of Disraeli's father.

Keep along the left side of the green, and at the bottom end turn right along a lane to a T-junction **H**. Turn left along a road, passing **The Red Lion**, and at the next T-junction turn right along the main road, in the direction of Aylesbury and Princes Risborough. After a short distance turn left through a metal kissing-gate, at a public footpath sign, and bear left to a railway underpass. Beyond, go right to the corner of a field and forward to pass through a gate on the left. Continue to the edge of the trees and after several paces the path forks. Keep left along the field edge, heading uphill to a gate in the top left corner. Continue up through

trees and in front of Nobles Farm, turn left.

Follow the clear, straight track along a fine wooded ridge for 1¼ miles back to West Wycombe. Initially there are fine views to the left across to Bradenham village, church and manor, with the thick woodlands of Naphill Common beyond. Later, gaps in the trees reveal pleasant views over the valley to the right, and in front the golden ball on top of West Wycombe church tower is soon seen.

On reaching a parking area near the church, bear right **J** and head across the grass to pick up and follow a downhill grassy path that leads off from the far left-hand corner of the car park. The built-up area ahead is High Wycombe. The path passes to the left of West Wycombe church, almost completely rebuilt in the mid-18th century, and the impressive hexagonal Dashwood Mausoleum. 150yds below it bear right at a path junction and after a few paces, at the top of steps, there is a superb view of the elegant façade of West Wycombe House. Descend the steps to reach the road opposite the starting point. ●

Chesham and Little Missenden

From Chesham the route proceeds through a quiet, undulating and off-the-beaten-track landscape of rolling hills, dry valleys and woodland in the heart of the Chilterns. The halfway point is Little Missenden, a delightful village with an interesting church in the Misbourne valley. This is a long walk with some attractive paths between Little Missenden and Hyde Heath and plenty of ups and downs, but none of the uphill stretches are steep or lengthy.

Chesham Although much of the historic interest of Chesham, a traditional Chilterns furniture-making town, has disappeared through the process of modern redevelopment, there are still some handsome old buildings and attractive streets near the restored medieval church. The former town hall building was demolished in 1965 but part of it has recently been re-erected as a clock tower and makes a striking feature in the pedestrianised High Street.

From the war memorial in the centre of Chesham, make for the mini roundabout and cross the road to enter Lowndes Park. After a short distance turn left along a broad, straight, tarmac path above Scottowe's Pond on the left, towards the church. In front of the churchyard entrance turn right **A**, at a public footpath sign, along a tarmac drive, later bearing slightly left off it to continue along a track into a field.

Keep along the left-hand edge of the field, beside trees on the left, and at the end of the field the path continues through trees. Emerging from them, bear slightly left and head gently downhill across a field to go through a kissing-gate on to a lane. Cross this lane, go through a gate opposite and walk diagonally across a field following the left-hand path to another gate and continue across the next field to go through a kissing-gate on to a lane. Turn right and, carefully following the Chiltern Link waymarks, ignore the first public bridleway sign to the left but at the second one, signposted to Herberts Hole and South Heath, turn left via a gate on to a track **B**.

Follow the track through the dry valley bottom of Herberts Hole. The track narrows to a path and runs between fields and wire fences. Beyond a junction the path widens to a track, then later dwindles to a path between hedgerows and wire fences,

Start
Chesham

Distance
9 miles (14.5km)

Height gain
575 feet (175m)

Approximate time
4 hours

Route terrain
Undulating downland, woodland and field paths

P Parking
Town centre car parks in Chesham

OS maps
Landranger 165 (Aylesbury & Leighton Buzzard), Explorers 172 (Chiltern Hills East) and 181 (Chiltern Hills North)

GPS waypoints
SP 959 017
A SP 957 015
B SP 944 020
C SP 924 024
D SP 923 020
E SP 914 017
F SU 920 989
G SU 929 990
H SP 931 002
J SP 946 011

with rising rectangular fields on the right. When the hedge on the right breaks, continue briefly beside woodland, then turn left at a waymark **C**. Follow an uphill path through the trees which bends to the right, to a gate on the edge of the wood on to a lane.

Turn left along the lane, ignore the first public footpath sign on the right to Redding's Farm, but at the second (half-hidden in a hedge and opposite a house), turn right **D** at a gate. Walk along the right-hand edge of fields, by a hedge and then a fence on the right, and where the fence ends keep ahead towards woodland. Go through a gap in

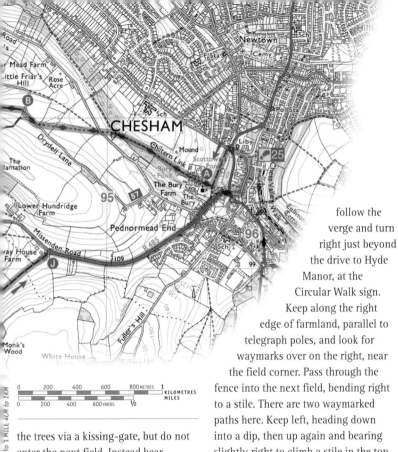

follow the verge and turn right just beyond the drive to Hyde Manor, at the Circular Walk sign. Keep along the right edge of farmland, parallel to telegraph poles, and look for waymarks over on the right, near the field corner. Pass through the fence into the next field, bending right to a stile. There are two waymarked paths here. Keep left, heading down into a dip, then up again and bearing slightly right to climb a stile in the top right-hand corner. Cross a track and take the path ahead to enter woodland. The path meanders along the left inside edge of the wood. Look out for where it turns left through a gap in a hedge into a field.

Turn right along the right-hand edge of the field and then, just before the field-edge bends right, turn half-left to follow a grassy path across the field. On the other side turn right to continue along the edge of Mantle's Wood on the left, heading downhill. Ahead is a lovely view over a typical rolling Chilterns landscape. At the corner of the wood, follow the path to the left across the field to enter the wood and continue through it, heading uphill. Just before reaching the far edge, turn right at a junction of paths to head gently downhill; look out for a white

the trees via a kissing-gate, but do not enter the next field. Instead bear slightly right on to a path that keeps along the left inside edge of some attractive woodland to a T-junction of paths. Turn left to continue along the right inside edge of the wood, go through a wooden gate and, following the direction of a Circular Walk waymark, turn right along a tarmac drive between houses. At a yellow waymark turn left **E** along a hedge-lined path, passing to the right of a bungalow, climb a stile and continue along the left-hand edge of a field, by trees and a wire fence on the left. Climb another stile, keep along the right-hand edge of the next field, by a wire fence on the right, to reach a stile near the field corner. Cross it – there is no visible path – and climb a stile on to a road.

Turn left opposite Hyde Lane. Briefly

arrow on a tree and a waymark post which point to the right. Cross a footbridge over a railway line, go down steps and walk along a path between trees and scrub, to emerge into a field. Keep ahead across the

The church at Little Missenden

middle of the field, climb a stile, cross the busy A413 and climb a stile opposite to continue along the left-hand edge of a field, by trees on the left. Cross a footbridge over the River Misbourne and keep ahead to climb a stile in the field corner on to a road by Little Missenden church **F**.

> **Little Missenden**   The church is one of the oldest and most interesting in the Chilterns. It was founded in the late 10th century and there is Saxon, Norman and later work. The main features of interest are the murals, especially the 10ft-high (3m) one of St Christopher which was discovered in the 1930s. The village itself has a sleepy and secluded air, despite its proximity to the London–Aylesbury road, with a 17th-century manor house and some very distinguished Georgian houses.

Turn left through the village passing **The Red Lion** and **The Crown** Inn, re-crossing the River Misbourne to rejoin the A413. Cross the road, take the slip road opposite which bends right in front of Lime Farm Cottage. Turn left at a gate to go over a stile **G**. On this next section the paths are narrow and likely to be overgrown in places. Continue along a path between hedges and wire fences and turn right. Turn left over a footbridge to re-cross the railway line and go through a gate. Continue ahead to a stile and then down the field slope, keeping woodland on the right. Make for the far corner to a stile and gate, continue ahead through the attractive Bray's Wood and climb a stile on to a road.

Turn right along the road through the modern residential area of Hyde Heath to a T-junction with **The Plough** pub along on the left. Turn right, and at a public footpath and bridleway signs turn left **H** along a broad tarmac path across a common, continuing along a rough track past houses. Follow this track which bends to the right to keep along the right-hand edge of woodland, and just before reaching a metal gate, turn right along a tree-lined path to enter White's Wood. Continue through the woodland, heading downhill, and on emerging from the trees keep along the right-hand edge of a field, by the edge of the wood on the right. In the field corner pass through a belt of trees and continue along a hedge-lined path to eventually reach a road to the right of Halfway Farmhouse **J**.

Turn right along the road for one mile – there is a footpath – back to Chesham. On entering the town bear left along Church Street, cross the main road, keep ahead and turn left by the clock tower to walk along the pedestrianised High Street to the starting point. ●

Chess Valley

The Chess is one of a number of small rivers that rise in the Chilterns and flow south-eastwards into the Thames Basin. This walk explores a particularly attractive part of the Chess valley, linking a series of villages – Latimer, Flaunden and Sarratt – lying to the north of the river, and one, Chenies, to the south. It is a varied route with some outstandingly beautiful woodland – especially along the southern edge of Chipperfield Common – grand views and pleasant, if sometimes muddy, walking across riverside meadows. It is also quite a hilly and energetic walk, though none of the climbs are particularly steep.

From the parking area turn left downhill along the road to a crossroads and keep ahead, in the Latimer and Flaunden direction, to cross the River Chess into Latimer, a small, pleasant village with an attractive green. Continue through the village and where the road curves slightly left, turn right Ⓐ on to a public bridleway (signposted Flaunden) enclosed by wire fences, which soon turns left and heads uphill to enter Long Wood.

At an immediate junction keep left, continue through this attractive woodland and on reaching its right-hand edge, turn right to walk along a narrow, hedge-lined path, later continuing along a track to a T-junction of tracks. Turn left and follow a straight, broad, hedge-lined track into Flaunden; the track curves right to reach a road just to the right of the Victorian church Ⓑ. Keep ahead to walk through the village passing **The Green Dragon** pub and at a crossroads keep ahead again along a lane signposted to Belsize and Watford, which curves left to a T-junction Ⓒ.

Go through the gate opposite, at a public footpath sign, and follow a path through the woodland of Lower Plantation, then continue along the left inside edge of the wood to go through a gate on to a lane. Turn right along the lane for ¼ mile through Woodman's Wood and, where it bends right, keep ahead Ⓓ by a barrier, at a public footpath sign to Belsize, to continue along a path through the wood. Follow the main path all the while, crossing over a path by a waymark post to continue along the left inside edge of the wood. After emerging from the trees keep along the left-hand edge of a field, by a hedge on the left, heading down to a gate on to a road at Belsize.

Turn left, take the first turning on the right and immediately turn right Ⓔ, at a bridleway sign, on to a path that heads uphill

Start
Stony Lane parking area, north-east of Little Chalfont

Distance
9½ miles (15.2km)

Height gain
705 feet (215m)

Approximate time
4½ hours

Route terrain
Frequent ascents/ descents, lanes, tracks and field paths

Parking
Stony Lane is just east of the outskirts of Little Chalfont, north off the A404 and the parking area is about ¼ mile (400m) up the lane from the main road towards Latimer

OS maps
Landranger 166 (Luton & Hertford), Explorers 172 (Chiltern Hills East) and 182 (St Albans & Hatfield)

GPS waypoints
TQ 005 981
Ⓐ TQ 004 992
Ⓑ TL 013 007
Ⓒ TL 019 011
Ⓓ TL 026 015
Ⓔ TL 035 012
Ⓕ TL 047 010
Ⓖ TL 047 002
Ⓗ TQ 047 998
Ⓙ TQ 043 993
Ⓚ TQ 038 984
Ⓛ TQ 030 990
Ⓜ TQ 015 986

between trees and bushes. Cross several drives and continue along wide tracks and paths on the southern edge of the thickly wooded Chipperfield Common as far as Apostle's Pond, a small pool just to the left of the path where there is a bench. This is an exceptionally beautiful part of the walk and the route is well- waymarked with blue arrows.

By the pond turn right **F** over a stile and walk along a path between a hedge on the left and a wire fence on the right. Continue between wire fences, bearing right to go through a metal kissing-gate at a corner of a lane. Keep ahead along the lane to the **Cart and Horses** at Commonwood, bear slightly right to continue along the lane, and at a fork take the left-hand lane **G** which descends through woodland to a T-junction. Turn left, then at a public footpath sign turn right **H** over a stile and walk along the left-hand edge of a field, by a fence and hedge on the left, heading up to a gate in the corner. Keep along the enclosed path. When it splits, keep right, pass between paddocks and tennis courts and then continue beside wooden panel fencing to the road. Keep ahead to a crossroads in Sarratt, a pleasant, spacious village with houses, cottages and two pubs grouped around a long green. The church, passed later on the walk, is ¾ mile away at Church End.

Turn right along The Green, passing **The Cricketers** and the village duck pond, and at a public footpath

sign to Church End turn left **J** along a track. Go through a gate and continue along the left-hand edge of several fields to enter woodland. Continue through the trees, later keeping by a wire fence on the left, and head down to a track. Bear left, negotiate a metal kissing-

gate and a stile, and follow a path along the left-hand edge of a field, by trees on the left. Where the trees end, continue across the field – there is no visible path – making for the tower of Sarratt church just beyond the field corner. The church is mainly Norman, enlarged over succeeding centuries, and nearby are a

pub and some early 19th-century almshouses.

Do not climb the stile in the field corner but turn sharp right **K** in front of it to keep along the left-hand edge of the field, by a hedge on the left, to a stile. Climb it and ahead is a superb view over the Chess valley. Continue

The River Chess near Chenies

downhill along a tree-lined track, and at the bottom walk across a field, making for a stile in the hedge on the far side.

Climb the stile and keep ahead, by a hedge and wire fence on the left, to go through a gate and descend steps on to a narrow lane. Turn left to Sarratt Bottom and at a T-junction turn right. Where the lane bends right, turn left, at public footpath and Chess Valley Walk signs, through a metal gate **Ⓛ**.

A quiet and pleasant section follows, through the Chess valley with the river to the left. Walk along a concrete drive and at the end of it bear slightly right to follow several stretches of boardwalk. Continue across meadowland by the river, following Chess Valley Walk waymarks, passing through a small area of woodland and finally reaching a lane. Bear left along the lane, cross the river and at a fork bear left up to a road. Turn left and then go up steps **Ⓜ**, and continue along a shady uphill path, parallel to the road, which curves right to rejoin the road. Continue uphill into

the village of Chenies, where church and manor house stand side by side in traditional fashion. The red-brick Tudor manor house belonged to the Russell family, dukes of Bedford, and inside the restored, mainly 15th-century church are several impressive Russell family monuments. Among those buried here is the Victorian Prime Minister, Lord John Russell.

Keep along the right-hand side of the triangular green and where the road bends left by a school, keep ahead, at a public bridleway sign, along a broad track. At a T-junction turn right and, opposite a concrete track on the right leading to Chenies Manor, turn left through a metal gate along a broad, tree-lined track. Go through another metal gate and follow an attractive path which runs along the side of the Chess valley, between scrub and bushes on the left and a wire fence on the right, with superb views to the right over the valley and Latimer village. The path enters woodland and emerges on to the road opposite the parking area. ●

Lardon Chase, Moulsford and Streatley

walk 27

Start
Lardon Chase

Distance
10½ miles (16.8km)

Height gain
970 feet (295m)

Approximate time
5 hours

Route terrain
Good downland tracks and Thames Path

Parking
Lardon Chase National Trust car park on B4009, ½ mile (800m) west of Streatley opposite National Trust sign 'The Holies'

OS maps
Landranger 174 (Newbury & Wantage), Explorer 170 (Abingdon, Wantage & Vale of White Horse)

GPS waypoints
SU 583 806
Ⓐ SU 581 814
Ⓑ SU 540 815
Ⓒ SU 544 826
Ⓓ SU 573 838
Ⓔ SU 576 836
Ⓕ SU 591 837
Ⓖ SU 593 836
Ⓗ SU 594 807
Ⓙ SU 589 807

A bracing start to this walk across the sweeping, empty expanses of the Berkshire Downs is followed by a descent into the Thames Valley. Then there is a delightful ramble along a lovely two-mile stretch of the river between Moulsford and Streatley. At the end, a steep but short climb to the highest point on Lardon Chase – 453ft (138m) above the Goring Gap where the Thames cuts through between the Chilterns and Berkshire Downs – reveals magnificent views over the downs, Thames Valley and Chilterns. Although this is a long walk, much of it is across flat or gently undulating country and all the climbs are gradual, except for the final one.

At the car park walk back towards the road, but before reaching it turn sharp right, at a public footpath sign, along an enclosed path which soon emerges on to the edge of a golf course. Cross the fairway and look for a track running between hedgerows. Continue across further fairways and near the bottom of the hillside look for a waymark, bearing slightly left to a footpath sign. Cross a tarmac track and follow the path to the right of houses to a lane Ⓐ, here joining the Ridgeway.

Turn left along the lane, which is tree-lined for most of the way, through the bottom of the valley for one mile. At the entrance to Warren Farm, bear right at a Ridgeway sign to continue along a broad track for another 1¾ miles. The track ascends gently and is tree- and hedge-lined, then it emerges into open country, with grand views over the Berkshire Downs. Soon after it starts to descend you reach a junction with a byway. Continue on the Ridgeway, keeping left at the immediate fork, and after 60yds you reach a byway sign and a sign -'except for access'. Turn right here Ⓑ.

After ¾ mile, just before a crossroads of tracks Ⓒ, keep right on a straight, broad, parallel, grassy track and follow it for two miles across the downs. This is the 'Fair Mile', traditionally used by horseriders for gallops, from which there are some wonderful views, especially across the valley to the right to the wooded ridge of Unhill Wood. Eventually the route continues along a single hedge-lined track to a road Ⓓ.

Turn right to head downhill – it is a busy road but there is a

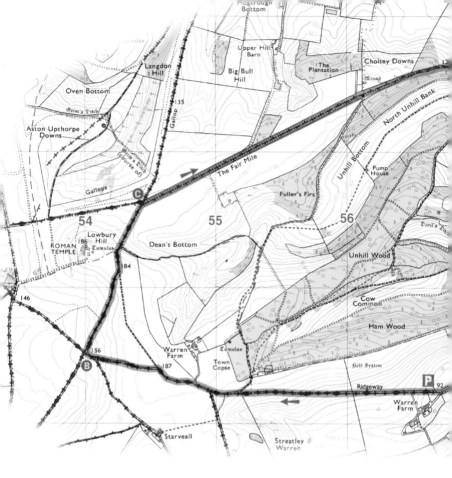

grass verge. Where the road curves slightly to the right, turn left **E**, at a public footpath sign, on to a grassy track that heads gently uphill across a field. Keep immediately to the right of the narrow wooded embankment, passing beneath the line of pylons to the very end of the thicket. Here look right for a waymarked gap stile, go through this and in three paces go right along the narrow path between fence and trees. At the end of this turn right (don't enter the recreation ground) along a path between paddocks and housing to reach an estate road. Turn left along this, keep ahead at the junction and pick up the track beyond the wooden railings, walking ahead to a road in Moulsford **F**.

Turn right, take the first turn on the

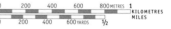

left, Ferry Lane, and follow it down between the buildings of the **Beetle and Wedge Hotel** to the riverbank **G**. Turn right to follow the riverside path for two miles to Streatley. This is a delightful stretch of the Thames, sometimes bordering woodland but mostly across open meadows, and passing Cleeve Lock; towards Streatley there is a particularly impressive view of the Goring Gap. Just after going through a gate into the final meadow, turn right to cross a footbridge on the edge of the meadow and continue along a shady tree-lined path which turns left and continues along a raised causeway into Streatley, passing to the left of the

medieval church. Turn first right and then left by the church to reach a road **H**. Streatley lies on the western (Berkshire) bank of the Thames where the river cuts through the Goring Gap. There are some particularly fine Georgian houses on the road leading down to the bridge, which links the village with its larger neighbour Goring on the opposite (Oxfordshire) bank.

Turn right through the village up to a crossroads and keep ahead, in the direction of Newbury. There is a pub - **The Bull** - on the corner. From here either continue along the road to return to the start or, for a more scenic finale,

turn right **J** after 200 yds past the Old Schoolhouse along an uphill track. At a National Trust Lardon Chase sign, go through a gate and bear slightly left to follow a path steeply uphill across the open grassland to a gate at the top. From here there is a magnificent view over the Berkshire Downs, Thames Valley and Chilterns, with both Streatley and Goring churches below in the foreground on either side of the Goring Gap.

Do not go through the gate at the top but instead turn left in front of it, keep by the edge of trees on the right across the top of the chase and go through a gate to return to the car park. ●

Princes Risborough and Chinnor Hill

Start	Princes Risborough
Distance	11 miles (17.5km)
Height gain	1,195 feet (365m)
Approximate time	5½ hours
Route terrain	Rolling downland tracks and field paths
Parking	The Mount car park, Princes Risborough
OS maps	Landranger 165 (Aylesbury & Leighton Buzzard), Explorers 171 (Chiltern Hills West) and 181 (Chiltern Hills North)

GPS waypoints

- SP 807 034
- Ⓐ SP 812 031
- Ⓑ SP 805 025
- Ⓒ SP 802 015
- Ⓓ SP 801 003
- Ⓔ SU 790 984
- Ⓕ SU 785 979
- Ⓖ SU 764 997
- Ⓗ SP 781 023
- Ⓙ SP 794 029
- Ⓚ SP 799 034

There is a definite feeling of remoteness on this peaceful, lengthy, hilly, but not particularly strenuous walk across a classic Chilterns landscape of rolling hills, beech woods and dry valleys. The route passes through three small villages, two of them little more than hamlets, all with interesting medieval churches, and there are superb views throughout. Undoubtedly the scenic highlight is the extensive vista across the Vale of Aylesbury from the Chiltern escarpment at the top of Chinnor Hill that comes suddenly and almost unexpectedly after emerging from woodland.

Princes Risborough Despite recent suburban expansion, Princes Risborough preserves the air of a small traditional market town with an attractive market hall in the centre and an imposing church with a prominent tower and spire, largely restored in the 19th century. Opposite the church is the 17th-century manor house, a National Trust property. The town lies below the Chiltern escarpment, surrounded by impressive scenery, and from many points the Whiteleaf Cross – cut from the chalk hillside to the east – can be seen.

Start in Market Square and, with your back to the church, turn right along High Street. Turn left at a T-junction and at the roundabout in front turn right along New Road, heading uphill. Just before the top of the hill turn right Ⓐ, at an Upper Icknield Way sign, to join the Ridgeway and follow a hedge-lined track which descends to the A4010 Ⓑ.

Turn left along the road – there is a footpath – take the first turning on the right, Upper Icknield Way, and follow the lane over a crossroads. At a Ridgeway sign bear left Ⓒ on to a path that heads across a field and go through a wooden kissing-gate. Continue between hedges, cross a railway line, go through another gate and continue downhill across the next field, heading for the left-hand side of a line of trees. Go through a kissing-gate, walk along an enclosed path and cross another railway line. Go through another gate and continue along a path, between hedges and trees, gently uphill across a golf course. Go through a kissing-gate and follow a fenced path between fields, passing to the left of an isolated house and on to a lane Ⓓ.

Cross the lane and take the path opposite along the left-hand edge of a field. Follow the curving field edge, climbing gently, continue to the top corner of the field, go through a gate and up the slope for about 70yds to the next gate and a bridleway sign pointing left. Take the path and continue along a broad, straight, grassy path, with lovely views over a rolling Chilterns landscape, heading downhill. At the bottom, pass through a hedge gap, keep ahead across a field, go through a metal gate and continue steeply uphill between wire fences towards farm buildings.

Go through a wooden gate to the left of the buildings and keep ahead to join a tarmac drive. Where the drive curves slightly right, bear left at a Chiltern Way sign, on to a narrow path, between a hedge on the left and garden fences on the right, and head downhill through an area of woodland to a stile. Climb it, continue downhill along the left-hand edge of a field, by a wire fence and woodland on the left, and then ascend slightly to a kissing-gate. Continue ahead, with a fence on the right, to meet a broad drive. Turn right and walk out to meet a road **E**.

Turn right, and then just past the entrance to Yewsden House, turn left through a gate at a public footpath sign, and walk along the left-hand edge of a field, by trees on the left, heading downhill; the path curves left to a gate in the field corner. Immediately turn right to follow a narrow, indistinct and possibly overgrown path that winds through an area of scrub and then continues steeply downhill along the right-hand edge of a field and through an area of scattered trees to a stile. Climb it, keep ahead through scrub and then continue to the next stile and then follow the path between paddocks to the road. Turn left downhill into Radnage, passing the church on the left. This delightful 13th-century building, noted for its wall paintings, stands in an

isolated position on the hillside presiding over the hamlet, which is little more than a collection of scattered, widely spaced cottages.

Opposite the lane which leads to the church turn right **F** over a stile, at a public footpath sign and Chiltern Way sign, and head straight across a narrow field to a gate. Continue across grass to pass through a gap in a fence on to a lane. Turn right and where the lane bends left keep ahead, at a public bridleway sign, along a tree-lined tarmac track. Where the track bends right through a gate, continue along a shady hedge-lined path as far as a T-junction. Turn left and continue along a tree-lined path which enters Sunley Wood.

Immediately turn right – the junction of paths is indicated on a tree trunk – on to a narrow path which heads uphill through the wood to a road. Turn left along it for nearly $^1/_2$ mile, and just before a left-hand bend turn right **G** along Hill Top Lane. Continue through woodland, passing detached houses and a row of cottages, to a parking area. At the end of this parking area follow the track to the left and then turn immediately right at a bridlway sign, to enter Chinnor Hill Nature Reserve. Continue along a straight path through attractive woodland, and on emerging from the trees a short detour to the left brings you to the magnificent viewpoint on Chinnor Hill, looking over the Vale of Aylesbury from the edge of the Chiltern escarpment, with Chinnor village immediately below.

Keep ahead along the path which now heads downhill into woodland once more. At a fork follow the direction of the blue waymark to take the right-hand lower path and continue downhill to a junction of paths to the left of a house. Bear right and in front of the house bear left, go through a gate and continue along a downhill track. Where the track curves right, keep straight ahead across a field towards the white building ahead which is **The Lions of Bledlow**. Pass through a hedge gap on the far side of the field, keep ahead past the inn and continue along the lane through this quiet and attractive village, passing to the right of the medieval church.

At a T-junction turn left and at the beginning of a row of houses turn right **H** along a track, at a public footpath sign. Climb a stile and continue along a tarmac drive to go through a gate. Keep ahead past farm buildings, pass through a gate and continue along the right-hand edge of a field, by a hedge and wire fence on the right, to reach another gate. Ahead, Whiteleaf Cross can be seen on the escarpment above Princes Risborough. Keep along the right-hand edge of the next field, to a gate and turn left to follow a path through a narrow belt of trees. The path turns right into a field; keep along its left-hand edge, by a hedge on the left, and where the hedge finishes continue straight across the field to a footbridge and gate. Keep ahead across the next field, later by a hedge and fence on the right, to reach a gate leading on to a lane in the hamlet of Horsenden.

Continue along the lane ahead, passing to the left of the tiny church; at one time it was bigger but the nave was pulled down in the 18th century, leaving just the chancel. Cross a stream, turn left through a gate **J** beside a thatched cottage, at a public footpath sign, and climb a stile. Pass to the right of a barn, negotiate a gate and follow a path across a field. Cross a stile and follow a straight tarmac drive

through the Princes Industrial Estate, passing under a railway bridge and keeping ahead to a road.

Cross the road and bear slightly left along a tarmac drive, passing houses, farm buildings and stables. Go under another railway bridge and then turn right **K**, at a public footpath sign, to follow a path across a field. The tower and spire of Princes Risborough church can be seen in front with Whiteleaf Cross beyond. At the far end of the field go through a metal

kissing-gate, descend steps, cross a railway line, ascend steps on the other side and go through another kissing-gate. Walk along a path ahead to a road and continue to a T-junction. Turn left and the road leads back via the church to Market Square.

Further Information

 Walking Safety

Although the reasonably gentle countryside that is the subject of this book offers no real dangers to walkers at any time of the year, it is still advisable to take sensible precautions and follow certain well-tried guidelines.

Always take with you both warm and waterproof clothing and sufficient food and drink. Wear suitable footwear, such as strong walking boots or shoes that give a good grip over stony ground, on slippery slopes and in muddy conditions. Try to obtain a local weather forecast and bear it in mind before you start. Do not be afraid to abandon your proposed route and return to your starting point in the event of a sudden and unexpected deterioration in the weather.

All the walks described in this book will be safe to do, given due care and respect, even during the winter. Indeed, a crisp, fine winter day often provides perfect walking conditions, with firm ground underfoot and a clarity unique to this time of the year. The most difficult hazard likely to be encountered is mud, especially when walking along woodland and field paths, farm tracks and bridleways – the latter in particular can often get churned up by cyclists and horses. In summer, an additional difficulty may be narrow and overgrown paths, particularly along the edges of cultivated fields. Always ensure appropriate footwear is worn.

 Walkers and the Law

The Countryside and Rights of Way Act (CRoW Act 2000) extends the rights of access previously enjoyed by walkers in England and Wales. Implementation of these rights began on 19 September 2004. The Act amends existing legislation and for the first time provides access on foot to certain types of land – defined as mountain, moor, heath, down and registered common land.

Where You Can Go
Rights of Way
Prior to the introduction of the CRoW Act, walkers could only legally access the countryside along public rights of way. These are either 'footpaths' (for walkers only) or 'bridleways' (for walkers, riders on horseback and pedal cyclists). A third category called 'Byways open to all traffic' (BOATs), is used by motorised vehicles as well as those using non-mechanised transport. Mainly they are green lanes, farm and estate roads, although occasionally they will be found crossing mountainous area.

Rights of way are marked on Ordnance Survey maps. Look for the green broken lines on the Explorer maps, or the red dashed lines on Landranger maps.

The term 'right of way' means exactly what it says. It gives a right of passage over what, for the most part, is private land. Under pre-CRoW legislation walkers were required to keep to the line of the right of way and not stray on to land on either side. If you did inadvertently wander off the right of way, either because of faulty map reading or because the route was not clearly indicated on the ground, you were technically trespassing.

Local authorities have a legal obligation to ensure that rights of way are kept clear and free of obstruction, and are signposted where they leave metalled roads. The duty of local authorities to install signposts extends to the placing of signs along a path or way, but only where the authority considers it necessary to have a signpost or waymark to assist persons unfamiliar with the locality.

The New Access Rights
Access Land
As well as being able to walk on existing rights of way, under the new legislation you now have access to large areas of open land. You can of course continue to use rights of way footpaths to cross this land, but the main difference is that you can now

lawfully leave the path and wander at will, but only in areas designated as access land.

Where to Walk

Areas now covered by the new access rights – Access Land – are shown on Ordnance Survey Explorer maps bearing the access land symbol on the front cover.

'Access Land' is shown on Ordnance Survey maps by a light yellow tint surrounded by a pale orange border. New orange coloured 'i' symbols on the maps will show the location of permanent access information boards installed by the access authorities.

Restrictions

The right to walk on access land may lawfully be restricted by landowners, but whatever restrictions are put into place on access land they have no effect on existing rights of way, and you can continue to walk on them.

Dogs

Dogs can be taken on access land, but must be kept on leads of two metres or less between 1 March and 31 July, and at all times where they are near livestock. In addition land-owners may impose a ban on all dogs from fields where lambing takes place for up to six weeks in any year. Dogs may be banned from moorland used for grouse shooting and breeding for up to five years.

General Obstructions

Obstructions can sometimes cause a problem on a walk and the most common of these is where the path across a field has been ploughed over. It is legal for a farmer to plough up a path provided that it is restored within two weeks. This does not always happen and you are faced with the dilemma of following the line of the path, even if this means treading on crops, or walking round the edge of the field. Although the latter course of action seems the most sensible, it does mean that you would be trespassing.

Other obstructions can vary from overhanging vegetation to wire fences across the path, locked gates or even a cattle feeder on the path.

Use common sense. If you can get round the obstruction without causing damage, do so. Otherwise only remove as much of the obstruction as is necessary to secure passage.

If the right of way is blocked and cannot be followed, there is a long-standing view that in such circumstances there is a right to deviate, but this cannot wholly be relied on. Although it is accepted in law that highways (and that includes rights of way) are for the public service, and if the usual track is impassable, it is for the general good that people should be entitled to pass into another line. However, this should not be taken as indicating a right to deviate whenever a way is impassable. If in doubt, retreat.

Report obstructions to the local authority and/or the Ramblers.

 Useful Organisations

Campaign to Protect Rural England
128 Sothwark Street, London SE1 0SW
Tel. 020 7981 2800
www.cpre.org.uk

Long Distance Walkers' Association
www.ldwa.org.uk

Council for National Parks
Tel. 020 7924 4077
www.cnp.org.uk

Natural England
Floor 6, Ashdown House, 123 Victoria Street, London SW1E 6DE
Tel. 0300 060 2634
www.naturalengland.org.uk

English Heritage
PO Box 569, Swindon SN2 2YP
Tel. 0870 333 1181
www. english-heritage.org.uk

National Trust
Membership and general enquiries:
PO Box 39, Warrington WA5 7WD
Tel. 0844 800 1895
www.nationaltrust.org.uk

Thames and Chilterns Office
Hughenden Manor, High Wycombe
Buckinghamshire, HP14 4LA
Tel. 01494 755500

Ordnance Survey
Tel. 08456 05 05 05 (Lo-call)
www.ordnancesurvey.co.uk

Ramblers
2nd Floor, Camelford House, 87-90 Albert
Embankment, London SE1 7IW
Tel. 020 7339 8500
www.ramblers.org.uk

Royal Society for the Protection of Birds
(RSPB)
The Lodge, Sandy, Beds SG19 2DL
Tel. 01767 680551
www. rspb.org.uk

Youth Hostels Association
Trevelyan House, Dimple Road, Matlock
Derbyshire DE4 3YH
Tel. 0800 0191 700
www. yha.org.uk

Tourist information:
Abingdon: 01235 522711
Amersham: 01494 729492
Aylesbury: 01296 330559
Henley-on-Thames: 01491 578034
High Wycombe: 01494 421892
Maidenhead: 01628 796502
Marlow: 01628 483597
Newbury: 01635 30267
Princes Risborough: 01844 274795
Reading: 01189 937 3409
Thame: 01844 212834
Wallingford: 01491 826972
Wantage: 01235 760176
Wendover: 01296 696759
Windsor: 01753 743900

Public transport
Bus traveline: 0871 200 2233
Chiltern Railways
www. chilternrailways.co.uk
National Rail Enquiries
08457 484950

 *Ordnance Survey maps
for the Thames Valley and
Chilterns*

The area of Thames Valley and Chilterns is
covered by Ordnance Survey 1:50 000 (1¼
inches to 1 mile or 2 cm to 1km) scale
Landranger map sheets 164, 165, 166, 174,
175 and 176. These all-purpose maps are
packed with information to help you
explore the area. Viewpoints, picnic sites,
places of interest and caravan and camping
sites are shown, as well as public rights of
way information such as footpaths and
bridleways.

To examine the Thames Valley and
Chilterns area in more detail and especially
if you are planning walks, Ordnance Survey
Explorer maps at 1:25 000 (2½ inches to 1
mile or 4cm to 1km) scale are ideal:

158 Newbury & Hungerford
159 Reading
160 Windsor, Weybridge & Bracknell
170 Abingdon, Wantage & Vale of
    White Horse
171 Chiltern Hills West
172 Chiltern Hills East
180 Oxford
181 Chiltern Hills North